Journeys of Race, Color, & Culture:

From Racial Inequality to Equity & Inclusion

Rick Huntley
Rianna Moore
Carol Pierce

New Dynamics Publications
&
NTL Institute of Applied Behavioral Science

Library of Congress Control Number: 2017941850

ISBN 978-0-929767-07-9

Printed in the United States of America

Graphic design for Continuum – Gail Beane, Laconia, New Hampshire

Printing & Graphic Design – Falconer Printing & Design Inc., Lisa Short, Falconer, New York
www.falconerprinting.com

For information write: New Dynamics Publications
Post Office Box 476, Laconia, NH 03247-0476
newdynam@aol.com
www.rickhuntleyconsulting.com

FROM THE LEADERSHIP OF NTL INSTITUTE FOR APPLIED BEHAVIORAL SCIENCE

As leaders of NTL Institute, we are excited to announce a collaboration between NTL and New Dynamics Publications. Our first venture is this powerful and urgently needed book, *Journeys of Race, Color, & Culture: From Racial Inequality to Equity & Inclusion.* It is a contemporary must-read book that delves into a complex and frequently misunderstood subject: racism in the United States. Despite our best efforts to see beyond skin color, our country continues the struggle to forge sustaining relationships across race difference, and even within our own racial identity groups.

Today more than ever, meaningful dialogue between People of Color and White People is the doorway to becoming the country aspired to in the founders' vision. Journeys is a major contribution to the development of that dialogue at a moment when racial tensions are at an all-time high. It examines the intergroup relationship between People of Color and White People by laying out our relational history and addressing the power imbalances and structural barriers that perpetuate institutionalized racism at the highest level – the US in its entirety as a social system. The authors are wise heroes who facilitate our movement into a decency that resonates across generations, and they are with us on the journey every step of the way.

NTL Institute was founded as a non-profit educational institution and has been at the forefront of Applied Behavioral Science (ABS) research and practice for 70+ years. The field of Organization Development (OD) began with NTL during the post-WWII era, at the midway point of the 20th century. Our mission is to advance ABS in service of social justice, oppression-free societies, and healthy individuals, groups, and organizations around the world.

Today we are a member-driven organization with members residing in all the world's geographies. As a leader in the learning and development field with high-impact programs that use modern experiential learning laboratory training methodologies, NTL continues to grow and contribute to the field. A premier training center in OD and human interaction in social systems, we develop successful leaders, stronger teams and organizations, and a more just and inclusive world. We offer programs in the US, Canada, the United Kingdom, and India, as well as in other countries. We are proud to bring *Journeys of Race, Color, & Culture* as the first offering in NTL's new "Engaging in Social Systems Change" series in service of our mission.

For more information, contact us at www.ntl.org | Twitter: @NTL Institute.

Karen Parker Thompson, MSOD
Chair, Board of Directors
NTL Institute

Rachel Pfeffer, PhD
Co-Executive Director
NTL Institute

James Smith
Co-Executive Director
NTL Institute

FROM THE LEAD EDITOR OF THE ENGAGING IN SOCIAL SYSTEMS CHANGE SERIES

Engaging in Social Systems Change is a book series authored by NTL researchers and practitioners. It incorporates solid research practices and theory with practice-based knowledge of Applied Behavioral Science (ABS) to offer new concepts, ideas, and options for encountering present-day systemic issues. Each book chosen for this series is provocative in its own right. Authors are encouraged to offer conceptual frameworks, models, examples, applications, and/or practices that result in positive change in our society. Each book addresses complex issues, provokes critical thinking, and offers approaches for meaningful dialogue. It is through the articulation of hard-to-discuss issues that the potential for changing behavior manifests.

We are pleased that *Journeys of Race, Color, & Culture* is the inaugural book offered to launch the new *Engaging in Social Systems Change* series. This book could not have come at a more critical time. A culture of power inequity, economic and structural inequality, oppression, and racism have led to fear-based aggressive actions taken by those in the general population (and some in role authority) who feel threatened by any movement toward social justice and oppression-free societies, such that our society is becoming increasingly polarized. Some might argue that we are at a tipping point where compassion, mutual regard, and honest engagement are being lost, perhaps forever.

NTL member-authors Huntley, Moore, and Pierce have researched and conceptualized the most comprehensive approach for developing an understanding of oneself, one's social identity and how we interact with others, and the damaging effects of implicit bias and judgment that one might hope for. Their book challenges us to learn more so that we can be decent with each other, gentle with ourselves, and nourish what brings us together. We could not have a better foundation upon which to offer NTL's rich history, expertise, and understanding of social change at a time when there is the greatest need. I find myself grateful for this offering of a constructive way to explore layers of difference in a conflicted world.

Kristine Quade, JD, EdD

Member of the Board of Directors, NTL Institute

Lead Editor of *Engaging in Social Systems Change* Series

CONTENTS

DEDICATION

We dedicate this book to all those who helped make the journey clear by sharing their stories and insights so generously. We appreciate also our colleague David Wagner (1939-2007) for all of his contributions over so many years, especially for bringing a White man's perspective to our work.

TRIBUTES

A tribute is given as a measure of gratitude and esteem. Derived from the Latin "tribus", it shares root origins with "tribe". We are grateful to these members of our own tribe for their tributes to Journeys of Race, Color, & Culture. They have used the Continuum in their social justice work in their various walks of life and as change agents in their workplaces, family systems, communities, and social/professional networks.

From the Executive Director of the ACLU Georgia....

The Journeys book and Continuum provide a resource which deconstructs past and present race relations and, more importantly, becomes an essential resource as we navigate the troubling times ahead. Scholarly analysis and case studies are integrated to not only facilitate understanding about where we are on the Continuum of equality and inclusion, but provide tools for successfully navigating a world which is increasingly multicultural. This book is important for both well-intended White People as well as People of Color who must constantly adjust to achieve in a world that is often uncomfortable with including them … or when they have been included by others. This is an important contribution which advances the Western multiculturalism project which began in earnest with the ideals and accomplishments of the Civil Rights Movement

--Andrea I. Young, Esq.
Executive Director, ACLU Georgia
Adjunct Professor, Georgia State University
Founding Executive Director, Andrew Young Foundation

From a Professor of Theology and Anthropology....

The authors of *Journeys of Race, Color, & Culture: From Racial Inequality to Equity & Inclusion* have created space for a dialogue in a country so polarized that it has become impossible to have reasonable conversations. This text, including the Continuum, provides insights about how racialized people (People of Color) and other historically vulnerable people are forced to live in subordinated status because institutions controlled by White People have power that is unlimited, uninhibited, and cruel. These systems have been further buttressed as the result of the election of a Republican President with a Republican Congress to support, and enact through legislation, terror for refugees, immigrants, Muslims, and of course (and primarily) Black and Brown bodies that have been criminalized via the school-to-prison pipeline, whose profit goes to the bottom line of the prison-industrial complex. The latter two dynamics are enabled by the 13th amendment of the United States Constitution that permits the enslavement of criminals. The descendants of enslaved Africans and undocumented Latinos who worked to keep farmlands in business are those who are enslaved: It is indeed slavery by another name.

The *Journeys* book and Continuum provide the framework, history, and analysis to help White people understand the privilege that has been passed down from generation to generation, and it helps People of Color understand the history they and their antecedents live(d) through and offer some knowledge of means to survive and thrive while moving through the matrix of race and culture.

This book is must reading for anyone concerned about where we go from here, related to re-infiltration of racism in the highest offices in this country.

--Linda E. Thomas, PhD
Professor of Theology & Anthropology, Lutheran School of Theology
Dr. Thomas was a co-author of the original Black-White Continuum

From a corporate Senior VP and Chief Diversity Officer....

Journeys of Race, Color, & Culture is a richly resourced book. On the one hand, it has applicability for classroom settings because of its historical accuracy and relevance in the current context. On the other hand, I have used it effectively and successfully across a wide range of initiatives in corporate settings, ranging from culture change efforts to one-on-one coaching. In a sensitive, balanced, and consistently positive manner, the authors deconstruct racial myths and tackle other difficult subjects such as racial power imbalances, the insidious complexity of inter- and intra-ethnic conflict, and White identity development, just to name a few. The book is presented as a journey, providing the reader with a map that is a picture of hope reflecting an evolution of what is possible at the intersections of race, color, and culture, if we have the tenacity to remain on the journey in an authentic way. Similar to other good pieces of literature, *Journeys of Race, Color, & Culture* will continue to stand the test of time, and I strongly encourage anyone who is serious about making a difference in their lives, or the lives of others, to read this book.

--Ralph de Chabert, Senior VP & Chief Diversity Officer,
Brown-Forman Corporation

From a team of organization development & diversity-inclusion consultants....

The insights shared from the perspectives of both White People and People of Color in this work are daringly honest. The corresponding, comprehensive Continuum masterfully provides an opportunity for self-revelation for those who are brave enough to reflect on their personal journeys in the world of cultural dominance-and-subordination. The work brings us face-to-face with that reality of inequality and offers suggestions for how people from both sides of the racial divide can work toward equality and inclusion.

Huntley, Moore, and Pierce "gift" us, both professionals and non-professionals who have dedicated themselves to eliminating inequality based on race, color, and culture, with this very powerful work to help us understand and move beyond fear and misunderstanding. It would be difficult to imagine one reading this work and continuing to say, "I just do not understand the problem" or "It's not my problem".

We have used earlier versions of the Continuum in our consulting work over the years as it has been very helpful in moving people into dialogue across race difference. Whether it is a one-time training event or an ongoing contract with an organization or community, we try to model the value of diversity by using a leadership team comprised of at least one Person of Color and one White Person. What has happened repeatedly when we are willing to honestly reveal places along the Continuum where we have struggled and moved forward or slipped back on the journey, the participants are more willing to share their own experiences. The language on this current version, along with its concepts and descriptive examples are incredibly rich, and we believe that many other diversity/inclusion practitioners will find it immensely helpful.

Jackie Bahn-Henkelman & Jim Henkelman-Bahn, Consultants

From an Organizational Effectiveness & Development Advisor at The World Bank....

From the very Preface, *Journeys of Race, Color, & Culture (JRRC)* captivates readers curious, intrigued, and aspiring to comprehend communal, corporate, and political life in the presently divided United States. More than just exposing the profoundly complex dynamics defining organizational and social relations, *JRRC* illuminates who we are as individuals, why we behave the ways we do in power relations with others, and gives expression to the deep and often unfulfilled yearning within each of us for acceptance, equity, and inclusion.

As a Caribbean-born, Catholic-raised, African-Asian Trinidadian gay man, I have had to relearn what it takes to live in America. My middle-class existence of educational privilege and accomplishment did not survive USA realities. It was in recognizing my own journey in *JRRC*, and teaching it to others in my client systems, that I came to appreciate, devise, and develop techniques for remaining alive and powerfully present in these United States.

The dynamics and theory that the *JRRC* Continuum expounds is the most profound analysis of what it means to be a Person of Color within the United States and beyond, empowering us with a way forward amidst the presently dispiriting chain of events.

--Lennox E. Joseph, PhD

Advisor, Organizational Effectiveness & Development, The World Bank

Dr. Joseph was a contributor to the original Black-White Continuum and served as President & CEO of NTL Institute, 1991-1997.

From an Organizational & Leadership Development Consultant....

Issues of race and social difference continue to fragment our organizations and society as a whole. We have farther to go in our journey toward equality and inclusion; this is important work that will take the commitment of each and every one of us. The *Journeys of Race, Color, & Culture* Continuum has been an invaluable tool in my own work. It is immediately accessible and understandable as it resonates as true from one's own experience. I encourage you to explore the Continuum. I believe it will bring insight and enable you to deepen your diversity and inclusion work in the world.

I want to highlight one point in particular on the Continuum that has most informed my practice: **"acknowledge the need to change and decide to learn"** led me to reframe my approach from helping people to change, to creating experiences that lead people to realize they need and want to change. These are "aha" moments in which people switch from being certain they are right to realizing the necessity and importance of looking at issues of race and culture differently. You see people from all backgrounds become more curious and open to learning about others' perspectives and experiences.

A particularly poignant example from my practice: I received a call from a friend whose 74-year-old mother had participated in a session I led on race in a church organization that was experiencing conflict related to racial divisions. The entire congregation was invited to explore the Continuum and share stories related to race. On the call with my friend, I asked, "How did your mother experience the session?" She said, *"My mother said', I know one thing after the session and that is that I have a lot more to learn about this. I've been looking at this the wrong way.'"* For me, this story shares the power of the *Journeys of Race, Color, & Culture* Continuum.

I believe we need more openness to others' perspectives and experiences across race difference in our society and organizations. *The Journeys of Race, Color, & Culture* Continuum is a deeply insightful tool to support this work. Reading the book is a personal invitation to deeply reflect on one's own work and to become better equipped to support others in their work.

--David Osborne,
Organizational & Leadership Development Consultant
at Change-Fusion (www.change-fusion.com);
Chair of the Board, NTL Institute for Applied Behavioral Science, 2014 - 2016

From the Founding Executive Director of Hope Springs Institute....

Reading this guide for a journey we all need to take and so often resist makes me hopeful once again about the possibility of creating an equitable and inclusive society. As a White woman, I was full of hope in the late 1960s when my husband and I adopted three African American children. I saw progress in the Civil Rights legislation of the time and believed that the world would embrace and support my children when they became adults. In the 1990s I lost hope and chastised myself for being so naïve. Then I realized my children would be part of the solution and took hope again. In these last few years, as the racist underbelly of our society began to show itself again, I felt nothing but fear when my African American great-grandson was born.

I believe this guide can help to make it safe enough for many of us to dive into conversations we would normally avoid. As I reflect on the places on the Continuum, I find myself having conversations in my head, sharing my stories, and eager to hear those of others. I want these conversations to be part of my daily life: to sit in a room with others to listen and talk and learn and feel.

I find myself eager to take the Continuum into groups I am working with. I anticipate risk taking, sharing, emotional roller coaster rides and deep learning that will change me, the people in the room and those we encounter when we leave. While working at Procter & Gamble in the 80s, I was privileged to do this kind of work and can see myself at all these stages, knowing I slip back again and again. I would have benefited from having this Continuum then.

I later dreamed of a retreat center that would foster learning and support equity and inclusion. Hope Springs Institute was born out of that dream and undoing racism and all systems of oppression has been part of its work ever since it opened. It is core to our Women's Leadership Collaboratives, the Agents of Change Academy, and our Certificate Program in Peace and Social Justice. *Journeys of Race, Color, & Culture* will be the perfect tool to encourage learning and seed the Capstone social justice projects.

--Suzanne Stevens, Founder of Hope Springs Institute (www.hopespringsinstitute.org)

From an Organization Development Specialist in Military Medicine....

The Continuum model illuminates our journey toward racial justice, offering an enlightened mindset about racial oppression and White supremacy in today's world. W.E.B. DuBois spoke of the "colorline" as the defining dynamic of the 20th century: Isn't it still, even in the 21st? Is that because reasonable people so quickly betray both their own interests as well as other human beings in their quest to move up one more tiny notch? The stark polarization between people at home, in the US, and the indifference of the masses toward immigrants – *human beings* fleeing their homelands to save their lives – would suggest it is so. The *Journeys* book and Continuum is a contribution to scholarship that connects social systems around race, class, religion, and more, as a wedge against maintaining destructive "them vs. us" social spaces that really only include the virtual 1%. It is a invaluable resource to consultants and change agents working toward social justice in their communities and organizations across America.

--Loretta Hobbs, PhD
Organization Development Subject Matter Expert for Highly Reliable Military Medicine, Booz Allen Hamilton
Prior to her current assignment, Dr. Hobbs was Senior OD Practitioner at the Walter Reed National Military Medical Center in Bethesda, MD

From a corporate organization development and diversity/inclusion specialist....

For many years, the *Journeys* Continuum has been foundational to my individual journey as a White person, as well as in my organization development work in corporations and non-profit organizations. This book's articulation of historic context as well as cognitive and emotional dynamics makes it relevant and useful in every setting in the US, with implications far beyond our borders. It helps me find compassion without complacency. I find compassion for myself and other White People in the understanding that our struggle to even *see* racist dynamics, much less work to dismantle them, is not because we are bad people but because we ourselves are enmeshed in this system of dominance and oppression. The compassion we have for each other helps me and us to journey on, choosing to learn rather than be immobilized by guilt and shame.

--Martha Comfort, MSOD, MME
Former HR Executive at Hewlett-Packard

From a founder and former Director of a K-8 charter school....

As the Director of a small, predominantly White charter school in the heart of a "minority/majority" state and city, I brought Dr. Moore in to help build the capacity of our mixed-race faculty to better understand race-culture differences and social dynamics in our system. In a series of professional development sessions, she introduced the Continuum chart and invited the faculty to explore our personal and professional journeys around race and color. Because the approach was oriented toward learning, no one felt blamed or shamed which enabled us to bring ourselves into wholehearted engagement. While exploring the personal aspects of our journeys with the Continuum as backdrop, we could see the institutional racism pervading our communities in terms of progress (or stagnation, as the case may be). This simultaneous examination proved extremely helpful for many of us who were unaware of the institutional impacts of race and culture.

The texts on the chart are concise and potent which facilitates rapid understanding of complex social issues. Another unique aspect of the chart is the way it parallels how People of Color and White People make progress toward equity and inclusion. This parallel positioning encouraged cross-racial dialogue among us as faculty, which furthered our understanding of the issues. We were able to expand our knowledge and deepen our understanding of how to build a charter school culture that fosters equitable and inclusive learning for both students and faculty.

--Kendra Toth
Founder and past Director of Mountain Mahogany Community School

From an instructional design project manager....

The Continuum is both simple and profound. I could immediately contextualize my thoughts and feelings as a White man on one path, and compare my experience to a parallel path for People of Color. Its clarity and meaning brought me to tears.

--Aaron Toth, Instructional Design Project Manager

From a lawyer and social scientist in the United Kingdom....

The *Journeys* Continuum was presented in an NTL Diversity Work Conference I participated in, in the autumn of 2015. As a European who has lived and worked in Africa and Asia for more than 30 years, I thought I had a reasonable grasp of diversity and inter-cultural human interactions. The presentation of the Continuum increased my awareness beyond anything I had previously imagined and highlighted areas that had been hidden to my view. I continue to use it and refer to it in my work.

--Mette Jacobsgaard, LLM & MPhil
Country Director, Kenya – International Development & Law Organisation
Mette is the founder of The Lincoln Workshop Series in the UK.

Some decades ago, I signed up for a Power Equity Group learning experience that was being offered for NTL members in Bethel, Maine. During that lab, I was introduced to the *Journeys of Race, Color, & Culture* Continuum. The staff of that program took me into their generous and generative holding container and gave me a life-enhancing gift. As a cis-gender White woman who was then, and still is now working in mixed race, class, religion, and gendered communities in the US and overseas, the equity-and-inclusion point of view about undoing systems of oppression taught in that lab has become a system of meaning that permeates my awareness and informs my behavior. It is always working within me as I practice my leadership and membership in all parts of my life, including the ways in which I hold my own family, friendship circles, my volunteer work in Hospice with End-of-Life care, and my dealings in this small rural community where I live. For those with the willingness and courage to undertake this journey, the *Journeys of Race, Color, & Culture* book and Continuum will serve as a wise and compassionate remedy for undoing racism and helping to create cultural islands of equity and inclusion.

Forever grateful,
Alexandra Merrill

PREFACE

Our purpose in offering this guidebook is to foster dialogue across the racial divide in the United States. Heartsick from the racist speech and violent events that occupy the news on a daily basis, we wonder how could this be us (the US!) in the 21st century and hunger to relate more effectively across race-color difference. How do we undo racism and internalized oppression, in ourselves and "out there"? The fact that you have this book in your hands suggests that like us, you also yearn for "a more perfect union".

Americans in the racial justice vanguard are already working to create equitable and inclusive social spaces in which race-color differences are seen *but not stratified.* In such social space, we would hold one another as equals irrespective of race-color differences and see each other as "normal" (mostly lovable, sometimes ornery) human beings. The racial hierarchy would be reduced to a cultural relic for anthropologists of the future to pore over instead of evoking the anguish that it does now.

This vision of equitable, inclusive social space is not mere Utopian wishful thinking for us (the co-authors here). We have practiced structural equity and inclusion in mixed-race groups of colleagues and clients for many years. We believe that U.S. culture overall has shifted toward greater equity and inclusiveness over the past few decades. The violence being perpetrated against People of Color in the contemporary moment can be attributed to White backlash against the increasingly robust movement of People of Color into the fullness of the humanity that is their birthright, and into institutional role power in all socio-economic and political sectors.

We are educators, coaches, and organization development practitioners who specialize in diversity-inclusion, culture change, and leadership development. Much of our life's work has been devoted to undoing racism. Our projects put clients on a journey where they learn to align their organization's culture with their avowed purpose and values. We work to heal wounds in the psyches of individuals, the strains in interpersonal and intergroup relations across race difference, and tears in the social fabric of the nation and its institutions that are the legacy of racism.

The Journeys of Race, Color, & Culture Continuum[*] portrays social power as a system of dominant group-and-subordinated group dynamics, mapping two theories based on observations of the power dynamics in organizations we have worked with:

1. An *individual's learning journey* focused first on undoing racism or internalized oppression in oneself and then learning to be equitable;
2. The *culture change process of a whole system* is portrayed by positioning the journeys of the culturally dominant group and culturally subordinated group in relation to each other, in movement from Racial Inequality to Equity & Inclusion.

"Subordinated" is synonymous with "subjugated" and "oppressed", terms that denote less-than status. A person deemed as less-than is denied access to resources and excluded from desirable social space. Violence is used to control less-than persons and keep them in their place. However, if your identity group is culturally dominant, you are given "more-than" status at birth which entitles you to unearned privileges, comfort at the expense of less-than others, and the right to use violent means to control less-than others...or *have others control them on your behalf.*

A social system whose culture is organized around dominant group-and-subordinated group dynamics[†] is intrinsically problematic because such inequitable power dynamics violate the UN's Universal Declaration of Human Rights[‡], not to mention the U.S. Bill of Rights. Thankfully, social systems are living, breathing organisms, energized

---

* Attached at the back of this volume for easy reference.

† We are talking about cultural hierarchies based on stratified differences between social identity groups, not organizational hierarchies.

‡ See humanarts@tc.umn.edu.

and in constant motion from the cultural forces within them. Like tectonic plates over molten magma, they are compelled to shift toward equity and social justice by the forces of resistance and democracy.

Evolution of the Continuum Concept

In the early 1980s, *newdynamics* innovated the use of a continuum to portray the learning journey of an individual or group. One day, Carol Pierce, a U.S. White woman, and David Wagner, a U.S. White Tuscarora man, were discussing gender dynamics. Carol claimed that she could plot where men as a group had been, what they had gone through, and how they had changed, based on the insights gleaned from consulting on gender issues in organizations. David stared in silence for a moment, then turned and left the room. When he came back, he had a piece of paper with a line drawn on it. The line showed where women had been, what they had gone through, and how they had changed[*].

Staring at each other for a moment, they exclaimed, "That's it!" They drew parallel lines, putting men on top and women on the bottom to symbolize their respective dominant group and subordinated group social statuses. When they finished, they had roughed out the first draft of what would become the *Male/Female Continuum*[†].

We would like to acknowledge other contributors to the evolution of the journey concept and Continuum framework, beginning with Heather Wishik who co-authored the book on sexual orientation[‡] with Carol, and others who contributed to what would eventually become the current *Journeys of Race, Color, & Culture Continuum.*

The first graphic on race-color was *A Black/White Continuum in White Culture: Paths to Valuing Diversity*[§], the product of a collaboration between Linda Thomas, an

---

* Carol observes that it's always easier to see the other person's journey than it is to see our own. We are usually very clear about what the other person needs to learn and how they need to change.

† Pierce, C., Wagner, D., & Page, W. (1986/2004).

‡ Wishik, H., & Pierce, C. (1995).

§ Thomas, L., & Pierce, C. (1988).

African American woman, and Carol Pierce. Richard Orange, an African American man, contributed key details. David Wagner created the basis of the journey for White men. Other partner-colleagues who contributed to its development were Barbara Berry and Diane Guy, African American women; Lennox Joseph, a Black Trinidadian man; Bill Page, a U.S. White man; and Karen Terninko, a U.S. White woman.

A *Black-White Continuum* was used for years in many client engagements. Over time, clarity emerged from the portrayal of the culturally subordinated status of Black People in relation to the culturally dominant status of White People. The *newdynamics* group realized that racism is an oppressive system that affects all Peoples of Color because of the colorism* endemic in U.S. culture. The Continuum was then revised to be inclusive of all Peoples of Color and retitled *Journeys of Race & Culture: Paths to Valuing Diversity*†. Several partners and colleagues contributed to its redevelopment: Sharon Bueno Washington, a U.S. Latina; Rick Huntley and Gar de Bardelaben, African American men; Kiyoko Kasai Fujiu, a Japanese American woman; and Martha Comfort, Jeanette Millard, and Rianna Moore, U.S. White women.

During the 1990s, Carol Pierce, David Wagner, and Rick Huntley began writing the book to accompany the Continuum. Doris Ferrer Roach, an African American woman, Kiyoko Kasai Fujiu, and Rianna Moore made substantial contributions. Readers at various stages of development included Nancy Brown-Jamison and Helen de Haven, U.S. White women, and David Blake Willis, James Regan, and Ted Tschudy, U.S. White men. Rianna Moore provided editing assistance.

Rick Huntley, Rianna Moore, and Carol Pierce completed the book, co-writing the text overall. We have listed our names in alphabetical order to signify the equity among us. Each of us took the lead for different chapters and backed each other up when we were not the lead author.

---

* Colorism is discussed in Chapter 5.

† Thomas, L., & Pierce, C., with Huntley, R., Washington, S.B., Wagner, D., & Joseph, L. (1999).

Collaborating across our own race-color-cultural differences on a book about race and racism has been both stimulating and challenging. We were compelled to deal with the impacts of our respective socializations in Black African American and White European American cultures, and to acknowledge worldviews shaped by life experiences differentiated by racial identity differences.

It "got emotional" enough at times to need a timeout but we always came back. Given our purpose, we knew we had to maintain connection and stay in dialogue. A "no-blame, no-shame" ethos helped with that. The struggle was a forge that tempered the mettle (pun intended) of our collaboration, deepened our collective learning, and continuously fired our passion for the project. Thinking together and feeling our way through sometimes generated insights that made it feel as if we finally understood everything, as if it was now all known and done, as if we were at the end of the journey. Then another episode of life experience emerged as we interacted, causing us to once again realize that a learning journey unfolds over a lifetime.

We always took time to reflect on what had happened during our work sessions. Reflection enabled us to sift through the grit to find any inspired nuggets of insight. It is hard work, and we don't think we're done. Given the nearly 400-year history of racism on this continent, we accept that for our lifetimes at least, the work is not likely to ever be *done*-done.

All the muddling and sifting deepened our collective knowing. The outcome is this book, including the newly revised and updated Continuum. We hope that it will support your own personal learning journey and the work you do to make the world a better place, for the highest good of all concerned.

Rick Huntley, Rianna Moore, & Carol Pierce

May 2017

CHAPTER

one

Introduction and Orientation to the Continuum[*]

Journeys of Race, Color, & Culture is a model of a social system undergoing a transformation. The system we have in mind is the United States because that is what we know[†] as lifelong citizens of this country.

The Continuum has been used since 1988[‡] in organization and culture change projects in corporate, education, government, and non-profit sectors. It is also used in social change and social justice programs in higher education. We wrote this book partly in response to requests from organization change leaders and higher education faculty for more depth and detail on the social system dynamics portrayed on the Continuum, but it is truly meant for anyone seeking a better understanding of these dynamics as they play out on stages across the nation in the contemporary moment.

RACE VEXES THE COLLECTIVE CONSCIOUS IN THE US, ESPECIALLY WHEN RACIAL DYNAMICS AND RACISM ARE HELD UP TO THE LIGHT OF DEMOCRATIC PRINCIPLES AND VALUES.

The culture change process is mapped as a journey on the Continuum, from **Cultural Dominance & Subordination/Racial Inequality to Equity & Inclusion**[§]. Embedded in U.S. culture since the

* A lap-size version of the Continuum is attached at the back of this volume, for easy reference.

† International clients point to the Continuum's relevance outside the US because of its focus on power.

‡ *newdynamics* Continuums are used by many other consultants in their client engagements.

§ Direct quotes from the Continuum are bolded the first time they are referenced.

pre-Colonial era, racial inequality created a cultural divide between White People and People of Color that persists to this day. Many people in the US are working to bridge the racial divide and change the cultural status quo. *Journeys of Race, Color, & Culture supports persons who seek to ...*

- understand the cultural status quo in terms of racial power dynamics,
- develop greater awareness and understanding of their own racial identity,
- undo racism in themselves and in their spheres of influence,
- participate in authentic dialogue across race difference.

Race in the United States

Race vexes the collective conscience in the US, especially when racial dynamics and racism are held up to the light of democratic principles and values. U.S. democracy is sometimes thought of as a long-term, social-political experiment that is continuously unfolding toward its promise of a level playing field accessible to all, irrespective of race or color difference. However, separate and distinct narratives about the true nature of the system have evolved over time. They are at odds over whether a level playing field exists in the US, and whether one is even possible.

The White culture worldview is centered on ideals and concepts such as religious freedom, individualism, American Exceptionalism, Manifest Destiny, consent of the governed, the rule of law, bootstrapping oneself, the level playing field and the meritocracy – a core tenet in this worldview, as expressed in the belief that anyone can succeed if they work hard enough. It disregards the barriers and hindrances imposed by structural inequality and racism to the life chances of a Person of Color.

The histories of the Peoples of Color* on this continent weave a different narrative, reflecting centuries of subjugation. The "rule of law" brought dehumanization,

---

* Anyone in the US who either *does not identify* as White or who *is not seen as White.*

economic devastation, great bodily harm, and death. Their narratives are rife with accounts of invasion, conquest, treaty violations, economic exploitation, forced removal to reservations and BIA* schools, mutilation, and genocide of American Indians; abduction from homelands, the Middle Passage, slavery, murder, rape, Jim Crow, savage mob violence (lynching, mass murder and the destruction of entire communities, church burnings and massacres), red-lined real estate, excessive incarceration and voter suppression of African Americans; abduction and forced labor of Chinese persons during the railroad expansion; the removal of Japanese American citizens to internment camps during World War II; the rhetoric of "self-deportation", "illegal aliens", and other exclusions of Latinos and Latinas from full participation and access; resistance to the resettlement of dark-skinned refugees from Asia, Africa, and the Middle East; the persecution of Jews and others considered to be less-than. Such catastrophes created innumerable barriers to the life chances of many generations of People of Color.

The tension between these disparate narratives has persisted throughout U.S. history. One remembers the utopian proposition that the US became "post-racial" by electing our first African American president: magical thinking, of course, as demonstrated by the explicit racism directed at President Obama and First Lady Michelle Obama as well as the overt and unabashed sabotage of his presidency† .

Let's imagine for a moment what life would be like in a post-racial United States. There would be equitable access to loans, decent jobs, housing, high-quality education and high-quality healthcare, irrespective of race difference. Voter suppression and racial-ethnic profiling would cease. No one would be stopped for

---

* Bureau of Indian Affairs

† The Republican leadership (Majority Leader Senator Mitch McConnell and others) swore to defeat President Obama's every leadership move during the first days of his first term; also, the incidence of death threats rose dramatically when Mr. Obama became president in 2008. In his first year in office, he received 400% of the death threats directed at George W. Bush in his first year (reported by the Southern Poverty Law Center).

DWB*. Race haters would stop assaulting African Americans, Latinos, and American Indians while shouting racial slurs. No unarmed African American males would be assaulted or shot by police. The numbers of African American men and Latinos incarcerated, or in organizational role authority, would approximate their percentage in the general population. African Americans and Latinos/Latinas accepted into university or promoted into role power would be assumed to have achieved on the basis of merit. People of Color refugees fleeing violence and death would be welcomed. People of Color would not be tokenized. White People would stop expecting a Person of Color to speak for their group, being surprised at how articulate they are, or telling and laughing at racist jokes. Contributions from People of Color would be recognized in meetings instead of being credited to a White Person later. Slurs, jokes, and stereotypes would land like lead balloons.

The nation's anxiety about race also colors our attitudes toward immigration. We like our nation-of-immigrants image but struggle with how to balance the right of those who came after our people did to pursue the dream with our wish to protect what we think of as ours. Do we welcome the "huddled masses yearning to breathe free" or build a wall?

How the Continuum Was Developed

Journeys of Race, Color, & Culture is an evidence-based phenomenological conceptual framework. Beginning in the mid-1980s, mixed-race groups in the corporate, government, healthcare, education, and non-profit sectors described the racism in their organizations, from individual acts of aggression to structural inequality and barriers to participation and performance that were rooted in racial prejudice. The Continuum took shape as the phenomena of daily work-life were documented. It was presented as

---

* Driving while Black or Brown.

a work-in-progress to many workshop and conference groups. A coherent and robust model emerged as their feedback was integrated over time.

Structure of the Continuum*: A Basic Overview

Journey Lines

The two lines that stretch across the length of the chart represent learning journeys for White People and People of Color, as groups. The journey for White People is on the upper line to reflect their culturally dominant status, while the journey for People of Color is on the lower line to reflect their culturally subordinated status. Their parallel positioning indicates interrelatedness and the possibility of intergroup dialogue.

The journey lines are jagged in the beginning to symbolize violence, conflict, and intense emotions. They become smoother in the middle to signify an inward focus and learning orientation. At the end, they join in a single loop that defines an open space or field in which race-color differences are held equitably.

Phases and Colors

The three major phases on the Continuum are presented in different colors. Cultural Dominance & Subordination is *orange* to symbolize violence, hatred, and fear. In the middle is the Transition, colored *blue* for a calmer acceptance of the need to learn and change. The *green* of Equity & Inclusion suggests social space in which access and the values of non-violence, participation, relationship, and social justice are the norm.

Top-Most and Bottom-Most Lines

The lines at the top and bottom of the chart represent the perpetual nature of certain aspects. For example, the extension of **White-Dominant Culture** well into the Transition represents its ubiquity; also, **Bicultural** extends the entire length of the chart to represent the de facto biculturalism of People of Color in White culture.

---

* In-depth descriptions of all aspects of the Continuum are presented in later chapters.

Movement on the Continuum

People of Color and White People do not move in tandem, despite the parallel positioning of their journeys. The typical pattern is for People of Color to move into the Transition first, with White People moving in response. Similarly, the journeys do not unfold in a linear fashion, despite the linear presentation. We move back and forth around the Continuum, depending on our experience in different social contexts.

Cultural Dominant Group & Subordinated Group Dynamics: A Power Analysis

A dominant group possesses more power, resources, and mobility than a subordinated group. The chart on the right displays a range of dominant and subordinated social identity groups on various dimensions of diversity.

Dimension of Diversity	Dominant Group	Subordinated Groups
Race-Color	White People	People of Color
Sex	Male	Female; Intersex
Class	Wealthy; Affluent; Upper-Class	Working Class; Poor
Sexual Orientation	Heterosexual	Lesbian, Gay, Bisexual, Queer, Questioning
Gender Identity & Expression	Cis-gendered	Transgendered
Legal Status	U. S. Citizen	Undocumented; Work or Student Visa; Refugees
Religion	Christian	Jew, Native American, Muslim, Buddhist, Hindu, Shinto, Atheist, other
Ability	Able-bodied	Persons with Disabilities

People usually identify themselves in terms of only one or two aspects of social identity (e.g. I'm German American; I'm heterosexual; I'm working-class; I'm Serbian; I'm Buddhist; I'm Cherokee-Choctaw; I'm a senior citizen). However, the reality is that each person embodies an *intersection* of many social group identities; for example:

- I am an able-bodied second-generation Italian lapsed Catholic trans-man.
- I am a bilingual dark-skinned undocumented Mexican woman.
- I am an elderly upper-class Protestant Lesbian descendant of the Mayflower.

Each of us embodies all our various social identities simultaneously, in any social context and from one interaction to the next. As the context shifts, a different identity "pops". Color may pop in one context and religious difference in the next.

This "simultaneity"[*] complicates interactions across significant social difference because our experiences of oppression are rooted in biographies that were shaped by the interplay among our various social group identities. Interpersonal communications get tangled in a web of assumptions, projections, and misunderstandings that are rooted in our respective culturally dominant group and subordinated group identities.

For example, an African American man and White woman co-workers can oppress each other in the same interaction. From the standpoint of her subordinated status as a woman, she is impacted by his sexism as he acts out male dominance. She is unaware of her Whiteness or its impact. From the standpoint of his subordinated status as an African American, he is impacted by her racism and sees her "acting White". He is unaware of his male dominance or its sexist impact. If they understand that they are interacting at both interpersonal and intergroup levels of system simultaneously and if they have the skill (and the guts) to stay with the tension and be open, honest, and direct with each other, they can name what's going on and explore it in the moment.

The chart[†] to the right summarizes a few manifestations of the power imbalance that affects People of Color and White

Dominant Group (White People)	**Subordinated Group (People of Color)**
Seen as superior, normal; set the standards	Seen as less-than; expected to follow standard set by the dominant group; discriminated against; needing help
See themselves as individuals	See themselves as a group
See People of Color as a group	See White People as a group
Have societal economic, political, and social power to shape laws, policies, and practices	Seek societal economic, political, and social power to shape laws, policies, and practices
Have unearned privilege (access to resources) and opportunity	Miss out on opportunities and privileges
Usually unaware of their dominant status; know little about themselves; unaware of White culture; see subordinated group as inferior extensions of themselves	Usually very aware of their subordinated status and in tune with their own culture; also know a lot about dominant group—necessary in order to survive subordinated group status
Hold onto their intentions, unable to see pattern in their behavior or consider its impact	Hold onto outcomes from patterns of discrimination and marginalization
Expect non-dominant others to conform and assimilate	Internalize dominant group beliefs about themselves; expect selves to conform

* Holvino, E. (2006).

† Adapted from Miller, J.B. (1976).

People, and their interactions. It can be used it to initiate a productive conversation across race difference, and keep it going.

The power imbalance is represented in the very grammar on the Continuum. The adjective "dominant" describes White People as the inventors of White supremacy. However, the past tense of a verb – subordinat*ed* – is used to describe the status of People of Color, indicating that it was done *to* them. They did not choose subordinated status. White Power is a power-over model, as in the orange section of the Continuum. It is still in play in the U.S. today. Its antithesis is power-*with*, the collaborative model. The power imbalance is but one source of complexity. Other sources are discussed below.

Other Sources of Complexity

Intragroup Diversity

Just as there is no unitary individual identity (one is not only Catholic, a Millennial, or Pakistani), there are no monolithic social groups. Each group is diverse within itself so any assumptions we make about what all Catholics believe, or how all Millennials act, or what all Pakistanis want, are likely to be off-base in terms of all the other diversities that each individual embodies on multiple dimensions of difference.

The Dance Between the Individual and the Culture

Culture can be thought of as the unseen structures that underlie a social system. Its force shapes the individual and influences behavior. At the same time, the behavior of individuals in social space reproduces culture. The yin-yang interplay of shaping forces between the individual and the culture is infinitely complex.

The Dance Between the Cultural Status Quo and the Force of Social Change

The status quo is a powerful force that drags on society's intention to alter a norm or practice that damages the common good, just like it drags on an individual's intention to change a bad habit. A culturally dominant group naturally wants to maintain the cultural status quo, so it reenacts dominance. A subordinated group colludes to the extent that it has internalized the oppression it has been subjected to. Socialization practices embed these attitudinal and behavioral patterns so deeply in us that we act them out unconsciously, saying it's "just how I am" if someone points it out, as if it were fate or biology. However, free will gives us the ability to make conscious choices about how to be, and how to behave, so we have the capacity to undo our socialization, if we want to.

*Social Constructionism**

Social constructionism is a worldview based on the idea that people co-create reality by interacting with each other. "Reality" is perceived as emergent and contextual, not fixed or absolute. If people say a thing exists and name it, they "construct" a reality. The thing may be concrete, like a Jersey barrier, or abstract, like field theory or the cloud. Validity accretes in layers over time as more people adopt the thing and its name. Eventually, it becomes reified (turned into a real thing) that exists "out there". Entire social systems emerge from social interaction in various environments. Think religion, public education, capitalism, the Industrial Revolution, the Electoral College, the bicameral legislature, and so on. "Race" itself is a social construction.

The idea of differentiated races† within humanity emerged in the middle 1700s, a time when people were focused on finding order in (or imposing order on) nature. The Swedish botanist Carolus Linnaeus, known primarily for his taxonomy of plant life, also created a set of racial categories, based on his observations of skin color and facial features. A German anthropologist named J.S. Blumenbach later remade

---

* This section draws on Bonilla-Silva, E. (2001); Frankenberg, R. (1993); Gergen, K. (1994); Gould, S.J. (1979); Habermas, J. (2001); Van Dijk, T. (1987); and Zinn, H. (2003).

† Modern science refutes this idea, asserting that biologically speaking, there is only one race: the human race. Further, differences in skin color, facial features, and hair texture are superficial and do not signify differences in either basic physiology or intelligence (Gould, 1981/1996; Zuberi & Bonilla-Silva, 2008).

Linnaeus's taxonomy into a hierarchy. His own biases regarding beauty and intelligence inclined him to set "Caucasoid" on the top rung and "Negroid" on the bottom.

The power brokers of the Colonial era then leveraged Blumenbach's hierarchy to rationalize slavery. It was the basis for a reinterpretation of Christianity that justified slavery on religious grounds. The entire U.S. socioeconomic system was, and still is, structured by the racial hierarchy. This is why the US is still "racial", not post-racial* in any sense whatsoever.

Implicit Bias

A final source of complexity is the phenomenon of "implicit bias". The notion that our perceptions of others and how we behave toward them are guided by biases harbored in our unconscious is uncomfortable to contemplate, and yet one social experiment after another has demonstrated the reality of unconscious bias and its impact on People of Color in a wide range of social contexts or interactions, from decisions about hiring and promotion to renting out an apartment to the skin color of a doll chosen by a

On Implicit Bias†

Implicit Bias refers to attributes or stereotypes that affect our understandings, actions, and decisions in an unconscious manner. These biases, which encompass both favorable and unfavorable assessments, are activated *involuntarily and without an individual's awareness or intentional control.* Residing deep in the unconscious, these biases are different from known biases that individuals may choose to conceal for the purposes of social and or political correctness. Rather, implicit biases are not accessible through interaction (emphases the authors').

The implicit associations we harbor in our subconscious cause us to have feelings and attitudes about other people based on characteristics such as race, ethnicity, age, and appearance. These associations develop over the course of a lifetime, beginning at a very early age through exposure to direct and indirect messages. In addition to early life experiences, the media and news programming are often-cited origins of implicit biases.

* Evidence for this claim may be found in the news on a daily basis.

† Kirwan Institute for the Study of Race and Ethnicity (www.kirwaninstitute.osu.edu). See also YouTube videos "Implicit Bias and Microaggressions" (Derald Wing Sue at Stanford), and "Unconscious Bias: Making the Unconscious Conscious" (at Google).

child. The Blumenbach hierarchy itself is a demonstration of the phenomenon of implicit bias.

An awareness of implicit bias is critical to the change agent's repertoire because it is a driving force behind our projections toward others whom we see as different from us. Various Implicit Association Test (IATs) are available online for readers to assess themselves*.

Racism can seem intractable, haunted as we are by White supremacy and the racial hierarchy, but it can be *undone* in micro-moments by engaging in constructive dialogue. "Race talk" can …

- raise awareness of our own implicit biases and increase interpersonal effectiveness;
- confront the behaviors and unravel the structures that perpetuate racism, and
- create equity in our spheres of influence, thereby shifting the collective consciousness over time.

The Continuum provides language tools for describing our experience. Without something like the Continuum to support us, we usually avoid talking about race, especially across race difference. (A lot of talk about race goes on *inside* racial identity groups, for better or worse.) Most of us would just as soon not "go there" because of some sort of fear. I may feel awkward or incompetent, worry about being inappropriate or not being able to control my anger or other emotions, or be averse to examining myself too closely. I may be afraid of the unknown, or of judgment, or of retribution.

Other Reasons for Avoiding Race Talk

There are two other social phenomena that keep us from talking about race, especially across race difference. First is the *tendency to associate with other persons who seem most like us.* Sociology's term for this universal human tendency is homophily, from the Greek: to love those most like ourselves. We gravitate to people

* The authors took the IATs on race and gender offered by Project Implicit at Harvard University (www.implicit.harvard.edu/implicit). More was revealed about our own implicit biases than we had assumed would be the case.

who feel like home. More taken-for-granted knowledge can be assumed with our home folk, so there is less explaining to do. A downside of homophily is that it hinders understanding and connection across social difference.

Second is *social distance*. Patterns of residential segregation set in place during slavery, Reconstruction, the forcible removal of American Indians to reservations, and the internment of Japanese citizens during World War II persist around the country. We may *feel* as though we live in a diverse milieu because we see so many mixed-race groups of office workers, hospital staffs, and police departments on TV. However, most Americans do not encounter different-race others until we join the military, go away to college, or take a job far from home.

Working with the Continuum

Journeys of Race, Color, & Culture puts a name to what is happening on our journeys whether we are a White Person coming from culturally dominant group status or a Person of Color coming from culturally subordinated group status. With the Continuum as a backdrop, we can identify and talk about our experience...

- bringing clarity to confusion,
- developing appreciation for multi-racial diversity, and
- managing intensity, release stuck places, and heal emotional wounds …

while preserving individual dignity.

The Continuum is *descriptive*, not *prescriptive*. It *describes* certain experiences *but does not tell us what to do.* Also it does not capture the entirety of any one individual's race-color experience, so to the reader we say: When something does not reflect your own experience, stay with your own truth. At the same time, we encourage you to be aware that content seen as inaccurate or irrelevant at one point can suddenly be useful down the road.

People of Color and White People enter at different points on the Continuum and engage with it differently because the differentiated histories of our groups cause us to bring divergent worldviews and unique frames of reference to our respective journeys.

Let's get to it.

When Working with the Continuum...

- keep an attitude of inquiry when it comes to others' experiences and perspectives,
- use it to understand certain social phenomena but not to judge or label others,
- assume that everyone is doing the best they can in any given moment and that everyone can do better in the next moment, including you (and us).

CHAPTER

two

An Orientation for White People

Chapter 2 is an overview of the difference that Whiteness makes, from word origins and power dynamics to White identity development. Written by White People* for White People, the first-person plural is used throughout to reinforce the idea that all of us (White People) are in this together.

DENYING OUR RACIAL IDENTITY PERPETUATES WHITE CULTURAL DOMINANCE.

We know how disorienting it can be to encounter the idea of Whiteness or our own White identity for the first time. We've been there. Our Whiteness privileges us White People to not see ourselves as White – to not see or own our racial identity, which is ironic because as a group, we are the ones who invented the whole notion of race to begin with, as discussed in Chapter 1. Our Whiteness also privileges us to expect others to see us as an individual and not lump us in with other White People, but in fact we all belong to the same racial group. We are White People.

The Scottish poet Robert Burns said, "Oh would some Power the gift give us, to see ourselves as others see us…."† People of Color often hold up the mirror for us to see ourselves more clearly, if we are willing to

* Rianna Moore and Carol Pierce.

† From "To a Louse" (paraphrased into modern English).

take a look. So, what is Whiteness, from the perspective of a Person of Color? Michael Eric Dyson describes it as a paradox:

> *... that even though whiteness is not real it is still true. I mean true as a force to be reckoned with. It is true because it has the power to make us believe it is real and to punish those who doubt its magic. Whiteness is slick and endlessly inventive. It is most effective when it makes itself invisible, when it appears neutral, human, American.*[*]

It's important for us to examine Whiteness and to see ourselves clearly as White People because we are preparing for a different kind of interaction with People of Color. We are embarking on a learning journey that will involve letting go of many of the assumptions, expectations, and stereotypes we've been socialized to from growing up in White culture, and – eventually – for meaningful dialogue across race difference.

A critical and necessary first step is to acknowledge the existence of Whiteness as a "force to be reckoned with". We may be surprised to discover how attached we are to Whiteness because we have been so unconscious of it, up until now. We are attached to the power, privilege, and comfort that have been the birthright of Whiteness for several centuries and many generations of White People. We resist acknowledging it at the conscious level because bringing it to consciousness means seeing how all of our power, privilege, and comfort comes at others' expense. But it has come at a cost to us, as well. We have had to "bear the burden of a false belief in [our own] superiority"[†] that has cost us the full measure of our humanity.

A close second step for each of us is to accept that we ourselves are White. It's not just other people who are White. We are not exempt.

---

* Dyson, M.E. (2017), p. 46.
† Dyson, M.E. (2017), p. 69.

The reality is that Whiteness lives inside us. We internalize it from growing up and living in White culture. No one alive today is to blame for this, exactly, but each of us here now is accountable for undoing the cultural dominance of Whiteness in our own spheres of influence, whatever they may be, however large or small, beginning with ourselves. Once we come to consciousness about it, we become accountable for it.

Our Whiteness also lives outside us, as when People of Color hold us in their gaze. They have no choice when it comes to seeing Whiteness. It is constantly in their face, for one thing, and they need to see it clearly and deal with it with alacrity and facility in order to survive. This is a literal fact in the US, not figuration or hyperbole.

It feels disingenuous to People of Color when we say, "I don't identify as White" or "I don't think of myself as White" or even "I'm not White!" How could we possibly not know we are White? Our denial erects a wall between us and them that keeps them from having access to our humanity and prevents us from seeing theirs. The sad fact is that such "them vs. us" walls keep us from having access to our own full humanity, as well.

It's easy to understand why a lot of us don't want to go there. Wanting to see ourselves as good people gets in the way of acknowledging our race because "White" equates to racism and White supremacy in our psyches.

We think we can absolve ourselves of the sin of Whiteness by pointing to our subordinated group status on another dimension of diversity (e.g. class, sex, gender identity, sexual orientation, ability, ethnicity, religion), as if being one-down on another dimension of diversity is the same as being one-down on the race-color dimension. Basically, we don't think that the race issue affects us much, unless it's our concern about backlash from People of Color for how badly we have treated them. We mostly see it as a problem for People of Color. We feel sorry for them and hope that racism "gets better" somehow, but we don't personalize it to our own lives.

People of Color know differently. Always critical of Whiteness, they understand racism as a collective psychosis suffered by White People with all its false illusions, neuroses, phobias, and hidden-forbidden desires. Once when Richard Wright[*] was living in Paris, someone asked him what should be done about "the Negro problem in America". He said that there was no *Negro* problem in America; there was a *White* problem.

We have been the problem since the Colonial-era White power elite leveraged the Blumenbach hierarchy to rationalize slavery – this is the critically intelligent view. Critical consciousness of Whiteness among White People began to amass following the publication of a seminal paper on White privilege[†] in the late 1980s. For us, being on the journey means acknowledging our race, learning about what it means to be White in White-dominant U.S. culture, and working to undo racism and White privilege.

The Syntax of Whiteness: Word Origins and Meaning Structures

Whiteness is a state of mind and way of being in the world. Rooted in White supremacy, it proclaims the God-given superiority of the White race and promulgates the idea that White People are duty-bound to "have dominion over" non-White others, as in "the White man's burden"[‡].

Coined in the 18th century as designations of race, "White" and "Caucasian" are often used interchangeably with "European American". However, these terms are not synonymous. White refers to race, not nationality, geography, or ethnicity. Caucasian refers to *geography* and is derived from the Caucasus, a mountainous region in the Near East[§]. *European* refers to geography and ancestral origins. It connotes White racial identity, although not everyone born in Europe or of European descent is White.

---

* Author of *Native Son*, *Black Boy*, *The Outsider*, and *White Man Listen!* among others.

† McIntosh, P. (1988). A white privilege movement emerged following the publication of this paper. It led to a White Privilege Conference (www.whiteprivilegeconference.com) in 1999, held annually since then.

‡ From an 1899 poem by Rudyard Kipling.

§ The Caucasus Mountains lie mostly in Georgia and Azerbaijan, between the Caspian and White Seas.

Nationality refers to nations. A White-raced U.S. citizen might have Argentine, Belgian, Chinese, Danish, Eritrean, or Finnish national origin, and so on through the alphabet to Zimbabwean, for as many countries as there are in the world. National origin can also suggest ethnicity, but there are many ethnicities that cross geopolitical boundaries to inhabit multiple nations or regions.

Ethnicity often overlaps with religion as numerous nations and ethnicities are represented in all the world's great religions. American culture(s) and nationality* exist but there is no American ethnicity. White Americans derive ethnicity from nationality, region, and/or religion. White racial identity, which exists in other countries, has a certain meaning in the US because of our history.

The peoples on the North American continent who were here before the arrival of the Europeans – American Indians or Native Americans; First Peoples or First Nations – are recognized as sovereign nations. They are focused in the contemporary moment on survival, recovery, self-determination, and cultural preservation.

The above paragraphs illustrate how demographic categories organized around *social constructs* like race, nationality, ethnicity, and geography often overlap and even contradict one another. Meanings shift as social contexts shift. However, Whiteness has consistently been held throughout U.S. history as a state of mind and a way of being in the world that are organized around power and privilege.

Identity Designations Used in this Text

We use a *racial* identity designation for White People and *geographic-ethnic* designations for People of Color. We want to be clear on our rationale for this apparent inconsistency (Rick joins us here to make this point):

---

* It is commonly assumed by many in the US that "American" refers only to U.S. citizens but anyone in any country in Central, North, or South America can legitimately claim American identity because they are from one of the American *geographies*.

- While there is debate among various Peoples of Color about how to name or rename themselves, many do claim that right and consensus has emerged in some communities to a) reject the race/skin color designations created by White People and b) name/rename themselves in terms of the geographic and ethnic origins of their people*.
- Whiteness is the binding force among persons from many geographic/ethnic origins in the world. It is a force that must be reckoned with by non-White persons across the US, whether they were born here or immigrated. Since we White People socially constructed Whiteness, including White supremacy, for ourselves to begin with, we are lying in a bed of our own device and dealing with it, here and now.

*De*constructing and *Re*constructing Whiteness

Some Persons of Color, working hard to differentiate themselves from subordinated group status, have asked what is left of Whiteness when its culturally dominant status is taken away. It is a worthy challenge to us, as White People.

In orange-section social space, during the first phase of the Continuum, our Whiteness is not a burden to us because People of Color are bearing it for us because we have forced it on them. It is in the early Transition (blue section) when this onerous burden shifts over to us. By acknowledging that we are White, we begin to assume the burden for Whiteness and take it off the shoulders of People of Color. We don't like it because it feels scary, painful, and tender, but we are stepping up. We can't stop being the color we are, but we can undo the culturally dominant status of Whiteness, which is to say, White supremacy. The Transition on the Continuum and much of what is written in the chapters for White People in this book is about how to do that.

---

* We believe in the right of human beings to name themselves. We also believe it is morally wrong and shameful to appropriate and caricature the names and images of culturally subordinated groups for sports teams and their mascots.

Once we have deconstructed the *meaning* of Whiteness, we can begin to undo the *cultural dominance* of Whiteness. Let's project our minds into some future moment when that task has been accomplished and ask, "What's left?" Is anything left of Whiteness after cultural dominance/White supremacy have been undone? Whatever remains could be the beginning of a *re*construction of Whiteness.

But wait. If the meaning of Whiteness is synonymous with cultural dominance and White supremacy, then the logical answer is that once you have taken those away, what is left is … nothing. We (Rianna and Carol) agree with Michael Eric Dyson, that "whiteness is a construct, an invention, that keeps white folk ignorant of Black life"* (among other things). We agree with Ta-Nehisi Coates that Whiteness is a dream we dreamed for ourselves†.

We dreamed it up to assure ourselves of our existential goodness, essential superiority, and righteousness. We dreamed it up as a screen onto which we can project all of our own "darkness" onto others whose skin is darker than ours. We dreamed it up as a talisman against our own heart of darkness.

Projecting our own heart of darkness onto others enables us to disown it. We can judge others for being "dark"; in other words, inferior to us, and bad. We absolve ourselves of the sin of darkness and relieve ourselves of having to do any work on ourselves. We set things up to simply eliminate or institutionalize darker-skinned persons when they act darkly, from the view of our superior "White" standpoint.

But when we step up to own and critically examine Whiteness against the values we espouse, we begin to be responsible for ourselves. This is a major developmental step for us as White People. Critical thinkers, both White People and People of Color, have undertaken a *critical naming* of Whiteness, as here in *Journeys of Race, Color, & Culture.* Whiteness is being subjected to a critical examination in various spheres

---

* Dyson, 2017, p. 58.
† Coates, 2016.

of social life, from the academy to religious institutions, to the corporate sector. At some point, "race" itself as historically constructed and manifested in the present day could be completely devoid of meaning. Race is a social construction, after all, so there is no meaning *inherent* to White or to any designation of race. All of us engaged in the work will need to stay tuned as we keep on keeping on.

Still: While "Whiteness" as a cultural phenomenon may someday fade – we can work toward it, and hope – our skin still has a color. As a designation of skin color, "White" is not really descriptive and may fade in popular usage. Already some variations of paler skin shades and tones are in use at the makeup counter: bisque, ivory, tan, beige, pink, coral, and so on. Not only that, but many White People invest a lot of time and money in becoming darker than their natural color. We disparage our "fish-belly white" legs and buy tan hose to mask them. Witness the folks baking on beaches around the world or in the "tanning" salon on the corner. Could it be that we are ambivalent about being White and pretending not to be, while still attached to the power and privilege of Whiteness itself?

Seriously, since we cannot really shed our skin color, any more than any other group of people can, we will only be able to show that dominance is no longer part of us by the character we develop and bring to our daily walk – how we let go of trading on being White. It is a long process for how Whiteness changes from being aligned with White supremacy and "white" becomes just another color. We know progress is being made when all skin colors reveal both external *and internal* beauty.

Whiteness and Power

A "power-over" condition is created when one social group carries out its will in opposition to the interests of another group (or prevents opposition to begin with). Power-over is different from legitimate power which is given voluntarily in response to expert knowledge, role authority, competence, control of information, or reputation.

White supremacy em*powers* White People to be *over* People of Color: to manipulate, coerce, and control them*.

White Identity Development†

White identity is an unspoken, largely unconscious understanding among White People of what it means to be White. It shows up in our attitudes, thoughts, feelings, values, and behaviors. It develops in stages, as summarized here in a stage model of White identity development.

Stage 1: Unconscious Acceptance	Stage 2: Awareness	Stage 3: Learning	Stage 4: Integration
Unquestioned acceptance of White-dominant culture values, norms, attitudes, and behaviors	Notice racism being acted out; witness its impact	Develop self-awareness and racial identity	Integrate being White with other aspects of identity
Oblivious to racism and White supremacy; it's just the way things are, the way things are supposed to be (i.e. natural order) OR Overtly espouse White supremacy and nationalism. N.B. Someone who espouses White supremacist ideology may either reaffirm their belief in that ideology or consciously reject and decide to learn when moving from Stage 1 to 2	Develop critical awareness; question White supremacy Overwhelmed; feel powerless; sense of guilt or shame Commit to social change Seek alliance with People of Color Depend on People of Color for learning	Acknowledge White privilege Learn about: *U.S. race history *Cultural Dominance & Subordination *other systems of oppression *how White privilege has influenced own life Connect with other White People to learn	Individualize People of Color; stop idealizing or romanticizing them Notice some White People working against racism Take on other White People acting from orange section of Continuum Become a race ally; teach other White People; lead social justice projects

The *Journeys of Race, Color, & Culture* Continuum supports our learning journeys through the entire process of White identity development by facilitating awareness of the true arc of U.S. history and supporting the universal human needs for self-actualization and community.

---

* Many of us do not want to be identified as White because we don't *feel* powerful owing to the wide range of class statuses among us, and/or we are subordinated on other dimensions of diversity.

† This section builds on the work of Hardiman (1982), Helms (1995), and Rosenblum & Travis (2012).

Conclusion

It is important for us (White People) to understand that undoing racism, whether in ourselves or "out there", is a lifelong project. There is no final state of enlightenment or done-ness in any permanent or absolute sense. There is always another layer to peel from the onion. We decide every day whether to keep on keeping on. How much can we persevere? How resilient and courageous can we be? What will we choose to do, how will we choose to be, everyday?

People of Color do double duty: dealing with racism everyday at the same time as they work to undo internalized oppression in themselves and in their communities. The difference is, they don't get to choose. We do: another privilege (or burden) of Whiteness. Once we accept this poignant reality, we can get on with the journey.

CHAPTER

three

White People in Cultural Dominance (Orange Section)

Chapter 3 is about the journey for White People in the orange section of the Continuum: Cultural Dominance & Subordination/Racial Inequality. The journey for White People comes first because White People, as a group, created the system to begin with and set standards for others to follow. People of Color react to what White People are doing in orange-section social space. The first-person plural is used throughout to reinforce our sense of collective, racial *group identity*. Overarching themes are touched on first, then individual locations in the orange section are explored. The authors are White People*.

UNDOING RACISM IS THE WORK OF A LIFETIME....

Overarching Themes

On the uppermost line of the Continuum, **White-Dominant Culture** extends across the orange section and well into the Transition to symbolize the staying power of White culture. **Fear of color** points to our reflexive fear of dark-skinned persons. We lock the car doors at certain intersections, cross the street when

* Carol Pierce, Rianna Moore, and David Wagner.

we see a Person of Color on the same side as us, and tighten the grip on our belongings in the elevator.

We go on the offensive to deal with our fear, using violence both preemptively and reactively to control People of Color. **Physical violence** in the early orange section shifts into **psychological & emotional violence** in the middle. This line encompasses certain acts of violence that are depicted on the White People's journey (more on that later). Violence morphs into **control & centrality.** We hold onto centrality and control to manage our fear.

Denial & projection are ego-defense mechanisms: a way of life for us in the orange section and well into the blue. *Denial* is the inability to acknowledge or identify our own emotions or to consciously perceive a threat as real. Denial allows us to avoid reality by denying it exists. We are in denial when we proclaim that race is not a factor in the murders of unarmed African American boys and men by White police. If someone questions our beliefs, assumptions, or practices, we deny that anything is wrong. We deny that People of Color have rich, full lives, separate from us.

Projection is the process of attributing our thoughts or emotions to another person, or blaming others for our own inadequacies. It takes place in the unconscious mind, outside awareness, and is basically a meaning-making mechanism used by all sentient beings to scan the environment for threats and resources.

Projection can bring structure, predictability, and a degree of safety to everyday life, but it also enables us to disown our fears, faults, and failures by "projecting" them outside ourselves onto others, and this is where the problem lies. White People unconsciously use projection to defend against our fear of color, which (to us) *is* reality, meaning that we believe that People of Color are to be feared and hated. We put our negative projections rooted in derogatory stereotypes onto People of Color to reinforce the social distance between us.

Our tendency to project so negatively onto People of Color is rooted in White supremacy and its pervasive, pernicious effect on our socialization and our psyches. Seeing them as less-than makes us feel okay about projecting onto them. It works like this:

When we are beset by inexplicable anxieties that we have no outlet for, we soothe ourselves by projecting them onto People of Color. When we feel inadequate or incompetent, we make ourselves feel better by projecting inadequacy and incompetence onto them. When we are terrified because a Person of Color is nearby (irrespective of whatever they are actually doing), we make them scary rather than owning how afraid we are. We point to how threatening *they* are as a way to justify our use of violence to control them or eliminate the threat altogether. Using projection to deal with our fear is only one step short of physical force; indeed, it often leads to physical force.

The darker the skin, the more afraid we are and the more we demonize the Person of Color, as in the example here. We avoid dark-skinned people whenever possible but if they are in our neighborhood or another place we believe belongs to White People, we challenge them. We're afraid of losing control and of backlash from People of Color because of how badly we have treated them. Such pathological fears

Projecting Fear: A Real-Life Example

A White policeman is sitting in his patrol car in a large U.S. city. It is night time. He calls to an African American teenager in a hoodie who appears to fit the description of someone being sought for a crime in the same general area. As the teenager approaches, the officer feels threatened and shoots him dead. In court, the officer says that he felt justified in shooting the young man because he "looked like a demon" and "was bulking himself up" as he approached. The shooting is later ruled justified.

wear the mask of hatred and infect our psyches throughout the orange section and into the blue, consuming enormous amounts of our emotional and psychological energy.

In the orange section, we are not conscious of attributing our emotions to People of Color but *they are highly attuned to this phenomenon.* They can feel the energy of our phobic reaction to them and avoid us as much as possible but are otherwise powerless to do much about it. If they should protest, we deny doing anything wrong and then go on to punish them – sometimes violently – for daring to call us out.

White Liberalism begins in the middle of the orange section and extends to the early Transition. White liberalism is a pose that points to our good intentions. We adopt it to cover the racism in us that we know is there. It makes us feel good about ourselves but does not require us to fundamentally change ourselves or the system.

White People in the Early Orange Section

The beginning of the orange section bears witness to the most heinous and monstrous acts of violence perpetrated by White People against People of Color. Our race group has used **genocide, race murder, brutal beatings,** lynching, and **rape** against People of Color to control, punish, and annihilate them. The White federal government ordered and engineered the **removal** of American Indians to reservations and Japanese Americans to internment camps for **containment** and control. The mass incarceration of People of Color by privately-held corporations is a modern-day manifestation of the same phobic drive on the part of White America to control, punish, and annihilate People of Color, and further, to profit from it as we have from slavery itself.

Violence provides a temporary release of the fear, hatred, and rage that simmer in the orange-section White psyche. The intense energy of these emotions creates an extraordinary atmosphere of intimidation that People of Color can sense in our presence. Intimidation also manifests in structural practices such as redlining real estate, informal segregation of public gathering places, and voter intimidation and suppression. Stand-your-ground laws and the White public's tolerance of police brutality toward People of Color give legal standing to all White People for intimidating and controlling People of Color.

In the earliest part of the orange section, White men are typically the active doers; however, White women play an important role by going along or goading on White men. Many White women collude by feigning innocence, averting their eyes, or not attending public events while others actively participate. Some White women socialized their children by bringing them to a lynching.

White People **sexualize** the **environment** to intimidate, humiliate, and control People of Color. It is a form of contempt, beyond simple disrespect. White men do it by telling sexual jokes or making sexual comments and double entendre. Besides thrusting sexual innuendo into everyday exchanges, they also make physical advances to intimidate and control Women of Color. White Women sexualize the environment by flirting and teasing a Man of Color to control him or play him off against a White man.

It is obvious that White culture is deeply conflicted about sexuality from how vigorously suppressed yet aggressively displayed it is. We **project hyper-sexuality onto People of Color** as a means of resolving our ambivalence. To the extent that we ourselves are uptight and over-controlled, we project wanton sexuality and immorality onto People of Color. We talk about African American men as "hung" and African American women as Jezebels, refer to Asian women as "oriental" (i.e. exotic-erotic; submissive) instead of the respectful "Asian", Latinos as "Don Juan" and Latinas as "loose". Further, a long-standing norm in White culture says it is okay for the White men and boys of the house to sexually use and abuse American Indian women,

African American women, and any Woman of Color domestic servants. Orange-section White men act freely on this unspoken norm while orange-section White women look the other way, or seethe with fury and take it out on the servant who is thus victimized twice over. This White culture norm was set during slavery.

White Men's fantasies about African American men as sexual predators in pursuit of White women inflamed their anxieties about having to protect the "purity and sanctity of White womanhood". Demonizing Men of Color permits orange-section White Men to rationalize their own rapes and debasement of Women of Color. Men's anxiety about their virility cuts across many cultures, to be sure; however, the superordinate hold that White men have on social power affords them a degree of control and access to the bodies of Women of Color beyond that of other men.

Driven by anxieties about their own virility, orange-section White Men have projected a superhuman kind of sexual prowess onto African American men and caused them to attack their manhood in horrific acts associated with lynching. Others who were not the direct target were intimidated and families weakened by such acts of sexualized race murder.

People of Color are **seen as inferior** by White People in the early orange section. White supremacists overtly proclaim that Black People are violent, devious, and not fit to associate with. Their polemics mesh with reactionary Christian beliefs that disparage all Peoples of Color. Some White People even see American Indians as interlopers in the lands that had supported their ancestors for centuries before the White man came.

Control is a serious pursuit and takes some doing, so we use **physical intimidation** to maintain White supermacy and cultural dominance. We create environments designed to intimidate and control People of Color. We define what reality is to ensure that we remain the locus of power and control.

At some point on the journey, we stop being physically violent against People of Color (it *is* against the law). Early orange-section White men now use **psychological and emotional violence** to emasculate African American men. Psycho-emotional emasculation can be undermining an African American man as he presents a project plan to the leadership team, focusing on an electronic device instead of giving him eye contact or giving him a hostile stare; holding side conversations; downsizing his scope of authority; taking a project away from him; taking his name off a work product he created. Orange-section White Women also use these tactics. Needing almost constant reinforcement of their sexual prowess and virility, White men of this ilk project their excessively violent sexual urges and anxieties onto Men of Color, especially those with darker skin. Commingled sex and violence are embedded in White culture at large but super-virulent in the psyches of orange-section White men.

We use **character assassination** to destroy the reputation or standing of a Person of Color in the workplace or community. We baldly lie about who a Person of Color is or what they did. We give feedback about them to a third party instead of directly to them. If concerned that our lie will be found out, we project deceitfulness onto the

Examples of Character Assassination

- "I'm sure she's doing her best.... Bless her heart."
- "No one *saw* her take anything out of Donna's desk but...."
- "I have a hard time getting along with him. I'm sure it's just me...."
- "*Some*thing happened at her last job but I'm not one to talk behind anyone's back."
- "He has a reputation for not showing up, but maybe he deserves another chance...."
- "He only got President of Law Review because of Affirmative Action." *This is a double whammy because it not only claims that he wasn't qualified but insinuates a lack of integrity. What kind of person would accept a job that he is not qualified for?*

Person of Color so they get in trouble. Character assassination allows us to justify privileges that we have not earned, blame others for our own wrongdoing, and avoid owning up to our mistakes.

Our projections rooted in fear and dislike extend far into our journey. If someone calls us out on a projection, we insist that it is the way we say it is. Half-truths and lies are how we act around People of Color in the early to mid-orange section, creating the micro-aggressions that ping on and undermine them all day long.

White People at the Midpoint of the Orange Section

We **project incompetence onto People of Color.** There is no way they could know what we know; there is no way they could perform as well as we do and be as capable as we are. We don't know what to say or do around them, so projecting incompetence covers our discomfort, which ranges from self-consciousness to mild displeasure to severe distress. Our arrogance and egoism reveal our fear of color.

Our **comfort and self-enlargement** come **at the expense of People of Color.** We keep ourselves up by keeping them down. They should know their place. They should not question us, display anger, or be too direct. They should discompose themselves if necessary. We want them to do things the White way. Our self-esteem is dependent on their accommodations. We are feel righteous because it is not our intent to hurt anyone. Neither do we want to know what our actual impact is.

Buried in our unconscious, resistance is a major block to moving forward. If we do not excavate and deal with it, it will keep us from entering the Transition. Down the road, from a point farther along on our journey when we look back at this dynamic, it embarrasses us to see how grotesque it is.

We don't like it when People of Color push back. Feeling threatened by their uppity-ness, **strong emotions** cloud our **reason**. Incapacitated by fear, our minds snap shut, thinking muddles, so we can't reflect accurately or listen to feedback. We restore our comfort and equilibrium by blocking emotion and reasserting control.

If our deepest fears are triggered, we strike back. **Retaliation** can be a sharp rebuke, turning away and giving someone the cold shoulder, or refusing to give eye contact. It can take the form of sabotage and have severe consequences: "forgetting" to share important information with a Person of Color, omitting their name from a distribution list, or insinuating something unsavory about them so they will be excluded from a desirable project.

Verbal intimidation includes threats, name-calling, loud over-talking, over-reacting, hostile questions, or using a nasty tone. "Do you have any idea who you are talking to?" "What do you think you are doing?" "Who do you think you are?" "You'd better watch your step." "That's just nasty." No matter how offensive our behavior is, we feel justified because restoring our comfort and reasserting control, power, and equilibrium is an imperative. The level of risk for the Person of Color is heightened but no matter: We expect them to stifle their anger or protest.

Orange-section White People accept that the Civil Rights movement was supposed to end segregation, but not effect integration. The end of segregation meant that we had to devise other tactics to keep People of Color in their place. **Exclusion** is one such tactic. Change the rules or meeting logistics but don't tell them; make the small print unreadable; make the "literacy tests" unpassable; split the community by building the highway between the church and the neighborhood. We prevent them from having access with a **lack of response:** Don't return calls; don't be available to meet; **withdraw** and put on the mask of White cultural dominance by shutting down our affect so they can't read our faces or body language.

Role-slotting People of Color into server and helper roles maintains our comfort. Someone might be an attorney, a university professor, or a corporate executive but we treat them as if they are a custodian, cook, secretary, maid, day laborer, driver, cook, security guard, or waiter. Our stereotypic role expectations diminish their dignity and self-respect but we don't apologize. That's just how it is.

We refuse to relate to People of Color co-workers as peers, nor do we accept a Person of Color holding role authority over us, no matter what the organization chart might say. We resist this role reversal and actively sabotage the individual to undermine their authority. We know how to immobilize someone and impugn their competence by hectoring them with a flurry of challenging questions and insinuating that they have failed. We **blame the victim** when our micro-aggressions cause someone to stumble. We do not acknowledge our part in any catastrophe that befalls them.

The darker the skin color, the more we **project** a **welfare image** (irresponsibility, laziness, deficiency), assuming the person is on welfare or has "a welfare mentality", irrespective of their actual economic situation. This projection is an undercurrent in any interaction between an orange-section White Person and an African American, Mexican American, or American Indian person. A Person of Color who clearly does not need assistance punctures and deflates this projection.

About here on our journey we begin to develop a conscience about U.S. race history and the race relations status quo. We are far enough along to know that it is morally wrong for one social group to subjugate another. **Guilt** begins to invade our psyche, causing distress and discomfort. Various circumstances and events can trigger our guilt (even shame), among them being called a racist.

About the worst catastrophe imaginable, being called a racist triggers a "neural hijacking*" in our brains so we are flooded with excruciating terror and anger. Feeling out of control, confused, stupid, unfairly judged, and misunderstood, we know that we couldn't be more wrong in others' eyes. No one seems to care about our

---

* Goleman, D. (1995). A neural hijacking occurs when a person's thinking function is overwhelmed by a flood of intense emotions, triggering the fight-or-flight response (p.14).

good intentions. Denial and defensiveness take over. After it happens to us, or we see it happen to another White Person, we withdraw and hide. We try to block the event from consciousness but it plays constantly: "Racist, racist, racist!" If we are aware of actually harboring racist attitudes, we don't dare talk about it because in our mind, it makes us kin to the KKK and other race-haters. We cling desperately to a self-image that we are not like those people. It is impossible to listen to feedback or learn in such a state.

White People in the Late Orange Section

In **White liberalism**, we see ourselves as someone who is helpful to others, a self-image that is central to our self-esteem. Being helpful protects us from feeling awkward with a Person of Color: "I don't know how to be equal but I can help you." Being helpful alleviates our guilt for the history and how much they have suffered. It means that we are not like the bad White People in the early orange section because we help others who are less fortunate. We interact more with People of Color now, but from a gracious persona, using gentility, courtesy, and niceness to cover our fear and discomfort; still anxious to be in control, but controlling through helping now.

Helping others is a strong value in White culture. It only becomes a problem when the impulse to help is about the White-culture expectation that as White People, we should always be stronger, smarter, and in control so we are obligated to help and assist lesser-than others. It is a problem when we help indiscriminately, without a context for what help is given, why it is given, or how it is given.

Do we check our assumption about whether the other person needs or wants help? Allowing them to decide for themselves about being helped is appropriate (they *are* an adult), but it embarrasses us to ask so we just go ahead and do it. *Indiscriminate helping perpetuates the subordinated status of People of Color* because in the end, it really is all about us and our need for comfort, control, and to feel good about ourselves. Having to check an assumption about whether help is needed feels like ceding control. They might reject our help, and if they do, we cry "I was only trying to help", shifting the onus onto them for misunderstanding our kind offer, or for being churlish. If we aren't allowed to help, we feel helpless.

In the late orange section, we learn to be "politically correct*" and hide behind a PC mask: If I say it just right, or keep my mouth shut, attention will shift off me and onto someone else. We don't know how to engage equitably.

We are hyper-aware now of other White People in the early orange section. The way they talk and act makes us extremely uncomfortable, and we do not want to be like them. When we were there ourselves, we joined other White People in the fear of color. Now, we avoid anyone whose actions are too outrageous and embarrassing.

The late orange section is a confusing place to be. We are ashamed about how badly People of Color have been abused, and chagrined to realize that the system of oppression persists in the present day. At the same time, we overreact if our entitlements are threatened. Undoing racism is the work of a lifetime because our socialization into Whiteness was saturated with it. In fact, we need to realize that there will always be an orange-section part of us no matter how far we have come in our learning journey. There will be always be times when we need redirection to consider whether our speech or actions have had a racist or oppressive impact, regardless of what we had intended.

We **tokenize** and **grant honorary White status** to one or two People of Color co-workers or friends whom we see as competent and socially acceptable. We justify our connection to them by saying that they are special, not like those other.... Accepting them assuages our guilt. However, we expect them to put their race-color identities,

---

* It is a common misperception that the notion of political correctness came from the diversity education movement. In fact it, originated in the backlash from people who were angry about being told that their speech was offensive.

pride, and issues aside in our presence and use their honorary status to keep other People of Color in line. If they refuse this role, they find out that they can be replaced.

Our comfort depends on how aware we are of our needs for sameness and difference in the people around us. Our thinking is muddled and contradictory, however. We like to focus on our similarities with others, but differentiate ourselves when that feels right. We want to be seen as an individual but also to fit in. We compete with other White People to be seen as better than they are, but when we are not sure of ourselves we want to be accepted by other White People because there is safety in numbers.

The question of sameness and difference also affects our relations with People of Color. We claim sameness when that serves us: "We are all the same under the skin," or "There is only one race: the human race!" However, in this context, sameness means Whiteness, and People of Color know it. We like to claim sameness when someone wants to talk about racism, which is why the sameness claim does not honor cultural differences. We feel good about ourselves when we claim sameness because we are raising People of Color up to White culture norms and standards if only for a moment. We don't understand that claiming sameness only privileges Whiteness, yet again*.

As we move toward the Transition, our common humanity is a given and we don't need to talk about it. We no longer automatically assume that People of Color are inferior or incompetent. We think that the safest and most respectful way to deal with People of Color is to **treat everyone the same.** Believing that we are taking a huge step forward, we pretend that race-color differences don't exist and adopt **colorblindness** as our stance.

Colorblindness works because it resolves the tension and discomfort of not knowing how to relate equitably with People of Color. It allows us to ignore White

---

* See Frankenberg, R. (1994) for further exploration of this analysis and argument.

cultural dominance, gloss over U.S. race history, and ignore the experience of People of Color who have lived under White supremacy.

Once again, we have purchased our comfort at the expense of People of Color. We sound righteous: "I don't even see skin color" or complimentary: "You are just like me" (read: "It's as if you are White!"). We are acknowledging their humanity, so it is an improvement over viewing them as less-than. We are at least trying to treat everyone the same. These mental gymnastics go on in our psyches, irrespective of what is actually happening. In the end, colorblindness does not make the differences go away. Instead, it perpetuates White cultural dominance, which is why it is located in the orange section.

At this point we are more confused than ever. What does it take to be a good White Person? We are in pain over our failed attempts to be good around race issues, so we **avoid** People of Color **out of fear** of doing something wrong, feeling like we have to walk on eggshells. We avoid People of Color by

- gravitating to other White People in casual gatherings or work groups,
- complaining about them to others rather than giving them feedback directly,
- not sharing information that would facilitate a task for them,
- avoiding their touch, such as in greeting or when receiving change.

At the end of the orange section, we still don't want to look too closely at U.S. race history, or at the real lived experience of People of Color, beyond what we imagine. We avoid examining Cultural Dominance & Subordination system dynamics too closely, especially looking at how our tacit acceptance of the cultural status quo perpetuates it. We sigh "It is the way it is," as if we have done all that any reasonable person could expect.

We allow some Persons of Color into our circles, at least superficially, if they present themselves in an acceptable way, but for the rest, **we wish People of Color**

well. However, they should not disrupt us in any way. They should work hard and pull themselves up by their bootstraps just like our ancestors did when they immigrated to this country. We overlook the fact that many People of Color did not "immigrate" voluntarily or were displaced from their homelands when White People came. We also ignore the boost of entitlements we receive from having White skin.

Unsettled at the end of the orange section, we sense that things are not right. Being made to feel helpless, inadequate, guilty, or ashamed makes us want to scurry away from the pressure of others' expectations. We see the need for social change but refuse to consider that we ourselves may need to change. We persist in individualizing ourselves. Our defensiveness is easily triggered. We imagine saying to People of Color, "Go do your thing. I know that it has been terrible for you people but I personally had no part in that. I mean you no harm, but leave me out of it. I am not going to change or do things very differently, so don't expect a lot from me." We worry that if we ally ourselves too closely with People of Color, we'll be treated the way they are treated. This dynamic is the last gasp of White liberalism and the final remnant of psychological and emotional violence.

We are right on the verge of grasping the notion that there is work for us to do that is not about helping People of Color. Under pressure to own our White identity, the individualism so steeped in White culture convinces us that our journeys are personal and shields us from the knowledge that the journey is going on at the societal level as well, and that we are a part of that larger phenomenon. We are not quite there yet. We give lip service to racial equality but do not yet completely understand what it means or how it applies to our lives. It is critically important for us to step forward into the Transition because our silence telegraphs assent to White cultural dominance.

The consequences of staying put and remaining silent are dire. First, it means that we are choosing to continue colluding in the racism and violence; second, People of Color will see us as choosing to be in the orange section instead of acknowledging their humanity. It is clear to them that we have not chosen the path of learning, engagement, social change, and authentic dialogue with them.

The Reverend Dr. Martin Luther King, Jr. said, “History will ... record that the greatest tragedy of this period of social transition was not the strident clamor of the bad people, but the appalling silence of the good people.” Our silence does not make us the good guys. Instead, it reconfirms that we are part of the problem. What are we going to do? Are we going to move forward on our journey or drop back into what feels familiar and comfortable – our culturally dominant status in the orange section?

CHAPTER

four

People of Color in Cultural Subordination (Orange Section)

This chapter illuminates the journey of People of Color in movement from Cultural Subordination toward Equity and Inclusion. The author is a Person of Color*.

"People of Color" refers to the multiple racial and ethnic groups, as well as some nationalities, who are commonly referred to as minorities in the United States. Minority group status is determined on the basis of a combination of the same or closely similar physical features that essentially designate that one is "of Color". Such features set this group apart from the racial group identified as "White".

Features that determine whether one is a Person of Color include (but are not limited to) skin color, hair texture, eyes, shapes of the nose, and body type. In the US, Persons of Color include African Americans, Latinos and Latinas, American Indians, Inuit, persons whose ancestry lies in Asia-Pacific continents and islands, and others.

As Peoples of Color, we took a proactive and assertive stance to distinguish ourselves from the

IT IS EXTREMELY DIFFICULT, AND OFTEN IMPOSSIBLE, FOR A PERSON OF COLOR TO TRUST A WHITE PERSON IN A SYSTEM OF RACIAL INEQUALITY.

* Rick Huntley

misnomer “minorities” when we innovated the terms “Person of Color” and “People of Color”. “Minorities” does not reflect the reality that collectively, we are the majority population in some areas of the US and the fastest-growing population in the US overall.

Having one term to identify People of Color implies a social connection among the multitude of groups. While some People of Color groups are sometimes connected socially, often they are not. It is more accurate to say that “People of Color” is a coded designation that informs as to who is White and who is not.

The cultural differences among and between People of Color groups are rooted in our respective histories, but the intergroup dance between us as a totality and White People is largely based on when and how we came to be in what is now the US. The theme that connects the diverse groups of People of Color is anchored in the social power dynamic between us and White People as represented on the Continuum: Cultural Dominance & Subordination / Racial Inequality.

Undoing culturally subordinated status in the system and in ourselves requires all Peoples of Color to navigate these power dynamics but our journeys begin at different points on the Continuum because of our differentiated group histories and individual biographies. Wherever we begin, our entry comes with the awareness of an inequitable, unbalanced power relationship with White People as the culturally dominant racial group. Irrespective of any social identity differences among us as diverse Peoples of Color, we all pursue equitable power relations and inclusion on equal footing with White People.

It is extremely difficult, and often impossible, for a Person of Color to trust a White Person in a system of racial inequality. If the myriad tensions and difficulties in our intergroup relationship are to be resolved and trust is ever to manifest, then both White People and People of Color need to take responsibility for making it different.

When everyone is aware of the racial hierarchy, it becomes possible for us to begin moving toward making the green section vision of equity and inclusion a reality.

Chapter 4 is about the journey for People of Color in and through Cultural Subordination in a system of Racial Inequality. Its narrative tells the history of how it has been for us in culturally subordinated status. The first person is used throughout: plural for the voice of the community and singular to stand for individual empowerment. Overarching themes, some of which extend beyond the orange section, are described first, then individual locations are discussed.

Overarching Themes

As People of Color, we know that our appearance is the basis for our group's subordinated status. No one has to explain this to us. From a young age (or whatever age we were when we landed on U.S. soil), we get that persons with our skin tones and features are not "as equal" as White People. Everyday encounters with White People continuously deepen the message that we are less-than. Sometimes we are told to our face that we are less-than, either by a White Person or another Person of Color.

All of us get the same message, irrespective of our particular racial or ethnic identity, so that we begin to unintentionally internalize the "you-are-less-than" message until it becomes an "I-am-less-than" message that plays over and over in our minds. As a result, we end up fighting each other over who is more less-than in relation to White People instead of collectively focusing the fight against the less-than messages directed at all of us by White People.

One terribly damaging manifestation of the internalized oppression we bear is a hierarchy of People-of-Color groups that mimics the hierarchy created centuries ago by White People, to rank us. Our version of this hierarchy points out which People of Color group is less objectionable to White People and which is more objectionable.

The extent to which we buy into this hierarchy reflects the degree of our collusion with White People to keep them up and keep us down, collectively irrespective of the differences among us.

The four lines extending across the bottom of the Continuum point to perpetual aspects of our journeys in subordinated group status. The bottom line asserts our **bicultural** competency. Our survival depends on our ability to understand and function in White dominant culture. At the same time, it is of paramount importance for us to nurture and protect our home cultures because they are the greatest source of sustenance for us as individuals. Home is where we get to be our most authentic selves. Home is the trusty ship on which we navigate our journey between White cultural dominance and our culturally subordinated status.

The bicultural line extends across the entire length of the Continuum to signify how endemic our biculturalism is. Being bicultural is a robust and resilient response to oppression. It makes us capable of flexing between, and operating effectively in, both White culture and our native cultures. Our biculturalism serves us well in the world.

As a group, we have survived in dominant White culture, albeit many millions of individual People of Color have died or otherwise suffered because of our culturally subordinated status. *There is no safety for us in White culture*. In the early phase of the orange section, our **physical vulnerability** and **psychological & emotional vulnerability** are profound because of the myriad forms of extreme violence perpetrated against us by White People. Whenever possible, we choose to have only **minimal interaction** with them and only as required by circumstance.

The minimal interaction part of the line comes at the point where the Transition begins. It is here, when White People enter the Transition by acknowledging their need to change and decide to learn, that we can be lulled into a false sense of security.

We can be so amazed and grateful for their new willingness to look at themselves that we begin to feel that we can trust some of them now (up to a point). But there are more unaware than aware White People out there. We continue to be at risk with them at the intergroup level until Equity & Inclusion becomes the new cultural status quo.

Anger & depression take up a large part of daily existence on our journey through the orange section and well into the Transition. The sources of our anger are multifold, from the failure of White People to acknowledge our humanity or to recognize that we have lives and priorities separate from theirs, to the violence that envelops us and pervades our existence, to the ways in which we are denied equal access to quality education, housing, and the voting booth. The cumulative effects of having to deal with all of this every day of our lives brings on depression. So many events activate our anger that we sometimes lose track of its source. Anger is how we survive. Anger and depression never completely leave us on the long journey toward Equity & Inclusion. In the latter stages of the orange section, the question we need to ask ourselves is: How can I handle my anger more productively to keep it from harming me or others? In the early stage, however, anger is simply a part of life. It just is. It boils and churns within us.

Depression is anger turned inward. It results from being damaged, dehumanized, and devalued. As long as we exist in subordinated status, depression remains as a residue left by the anger that is buried inside and carried there over time. We are often unaware of the multiple ways in which anger and depression affect us in terms of the long-term effects on mental and physical health and overall well-being.

The anger and injuries that so fill our lives make us **guarded**. We resist opening up and sharing ourselves because of the hurt and anger, especially when curious White People bombard us with questions and demands. Our guardedness protects us in the early orange section against abuse, violence, and messages that we are less-than. It persists well into the Transition.

We have a lot to guard against, beyond being bombarded with questions. White People's unwillingness to acknowledge the dominance of Whiteness and its impacts. Our psychological and emotional vulnerability – we are vulnerable on these dimensions because White People continue to perpetrate psychological and emotional violence against us. Guardedness is so imbued in us that we rarely individualize White People, thus we guard ourselves indiscriminately against all of them. With other People of Color, we may hide how hurt we are, but we do not guard against who we are.

Guardedness is a mostly unconscious method of survival. As we move toward the Transition, we gradually relax our guard and become more particular about what we need to guard against. Self-protectiveness as a habit of being has been entrenched so deeply in our psyches that now we need to create new ways to express ourselves, especially our experiences around race, color, and ethnicity.

The ultimate cost of guardedness is this: *Guardedness renders us invisible* to *White People because it masks our authentic selves.* If we only react to what is outside of us, our authentic inner self becomes inaccessible, not only to others but to ourselves. The danger of being too guarded, or of being guarded for too long, is that we can lose our unique and precious selves entirely.

The final overarching theme points to our major job for surviving subordinated status, which is to **keep White People comfortable.** We manipulate circumstances to keep them comfortable; at great cost to ourselves, however, especially when they negate us even as we exert ourselves to prevent any disturbance for them. It takes an enormous amount of our time and energy, leaving little for us to work with on our own behalf with whatever remains of our lives. But if we don't do it, we don't survive.

The earlier we are in Cultural Dominance & Subordination, the less we question our subordinated status, and the more painful it is to admit collusion. Whatever we have done, it was only what was needed to survive. We may not yet be aware of existing in a system of oppression, even as we labor under the yoke of subordinated status. The violence that orange-section White People perpetrate against us limits our life chances and prevents us from being in control of our own lives. Anger, depression, and guardedness are predictable and reasonable responses to such conditions.

People of Color in the Early Orange Section

It is easy for us to externalize our anger and rage at the violence perpetrated against us by resorting to violence ourselves. Once we reach containment capacity, we may strike out at White supremacist behavior, at the artifacts that depict White supremacy, or at the perpetrators themselves. Anything White represents the oppressor.

Striking back at White supremacy is not likely to result in either success or survival. Indeed, striking back can well be looked on as a suicidal act. However, *the suicidal wish that accompanies an* ***explosion to violence*** *against White People is less about a wish to die and more about a desire to stop the pain.* If we survive an explosion to violence, then the release we feel enables us to exist awhile longer.

Extreme violence between People of Color is called **horizontal violence.** When the capacity to contain our anger has exceeded its limits, *we lash out at others who look like us* or whom we view as also subordinated racially. We know that we cannot lash out at White People – the actual perpetrators – because that would be too dangerous. They are the dominant group. Therefore, we lash out at others like us, even though their actions are not the true source of our rage.

We survive through **denial**. Denial enables us to overlook the injustice that pervades our lives. We deny that we are the subordinated group in a system of oppression, a reality that feels too overwhelming to admit to ourselves. We call injustice and oppression by some other name to pretend that it is something other than what it is. We want it to be anything other than racism and White supremacy.

Denial helps us to survive from one day to the next until finally it becomes a way of life. It works because it numbs us out. Over time, however, it takes a physical, emotional, and spiritual toll. The deterioration of our well-being and deadening of our soul means that we can't show up and be fully present in our communities as whole, integrated, energized persons ready and able to protect, serve, support, and lead.

Denial is also useful because it is something other than anger or depression to preoccupy ourselves with. As a container for anger and depression, denial can enable us to survive and create a reasonable existence for ourselves because the container of denial is helping us to compartmentalize our experience. It makes it possible for us to not have to look too closely at the bad parts too much of the time. We live damaged, inauthentic lives in order to survive, but the price is our wholeness.

Being subordinated requires us to carry our individual anger at oppression and injustice *in addition* to the historical, collective anger of our entire subordinated race group in White-dominant culture. When anger goes unacknowledged and unresolved for too long, it transmutes into **rage turned inward.** Rage can explode outward as violence directed at others or turned inward, a missile aimed at one's own heart, soul, and psyche. It inflicts extreme pain from its massive destructive power. Once our resistance and resilience have been drained off completely, with no end to the oppression in sight, we self-medicate to get through it, resorting to substances outside ourselves to find relief.

Substance abuse and other self-defeating behaviors such as excessive eating or drinking, gambling, abusing drugs, or driving recklessly, drive the pain underground and prolong the numbing that is so needed to survive. Food, drugs (licit and illicit), and alcohol are substances that we can control … until we can't, and they control us.

In the short-term, **addiction** comforts and soothes by providing momentary relief from the existential pain. Our subconscious knows that we are hurting ourselves and the people who love us but we keep doing it because it is how we survive. We isolate from White People to further punish ourselves with self-talk like "I'm not good enough," "I'm not qualified enough," or "I'm not deserving enough."

When the culture abandons us completely and all hope is gone, the will to live fades and at some point departs the psyche altogether. It is at this point that we turn to suicide. More has been laid upon us than we can handle; no help is on the horizon; no end is in sight. Some of us commit the act outright but if the terror of that final aloneness is outside conscious awareness we may instead put ourselves in harm's way by engaging in behavior that has lethal consequences.

Shame about physical characteristics is deeply embedded in our psyches because White People see our bodies as ugly and undesirable. Their abhorrence creates shame and embarrassment in us for who we are because Whiteness is culturally dominant. White standards of beauty saturate the airwaves, broadcasting the message that our bodies and features are too big, too thin, too broad or too small; our skin is too dark; our eyes are too slanted or not round enough; our hair is too kinky, too curly, too dark, too coarse or too straight, and so on. Children internalize this shame at an early age, rejecting dolls that look like them and choosing White dolls to play with, just as adults choose White role models for how to be beautiful.

We are driven to drastic measures, even surgery, to radically alter certain aspects of our appearance that are typical of our ethnicity. Camouflaging our cultural characteristics foments **self-hatred**. We despise ourselves and others like us. Given such low regard for our racial identity, cultural history, and appearance, we begin to **fabricate reality** as a way to deal with it. We see the access that White People have to opportunities and resources that are either denied us or that we have to work twice as hard for, so we attempt to make up for such disadvantages in hopes of being accepted. We manufacture stories about ourselves and our history, often omitting or minimizing truths about our real-life experiences, both historic and present day (e.g. slavery, genocide, adopting White culture images and ideas about our group and our culture).

Fabricating reality is an attempt to level the playing field with White People, even as we realize that they built the field. We smile and laugh to mask our hurt or anger and fear of being identified with our race-color group which is so inadequate to our eyes. This reality is harsh to admit to ourselves, but nonetheless true. Fabricating reality is one more way to be in denial because it camouflages our fear about who we really are.

We also fabricate reality for White People when we allow them to believe that we are fine with the way things are. We do not tell them the truth about the impact of White dominance on us. Withholding these truths helps to keep White People comfortable because it takes them off the hook so they don't have to worry or be upset.

We get to the point where we believe that things will never change. We reconcile ourselves to subordinated group status and rationalize it as the way it's supposed to be. This dynamic is at the core of colluding to maintain White dominance – a truly toxic and dangerous dynamic for us as People of Color because it leads to blaming ourselves for the adversity we face, instead of looking critically at the system. We act as if success is a White phenomenon, explaining tortuously and shamefully how we brought our failures upon ourselves. Every time we do this, the hole of subordinated status gets dug a little deeper. After a while, there's not much we can do to get out of it. The sense of being less-than pervades everything we think, feel, and do.

Paradoxically, we also know that nothing good happens in our lives unless we do something for ourselves. Knowing this prompts us to take responsibility for the changes that need to be made in our lives. We admire the person who pulls themselves up by their bootstraps but ignore how someone is always stealing our boots. Or we excuse a White person for committing a micro-aggression by saying "He did not mean any harm; he's really a nice person." We assume benign intent and fail to demand accountability from the White person for his or her language and behavior and their impacts.

Rationalizing our subordinated group status means that we accept and internalize others' views and definitions of us as true for our racial identity group, community, and culture in its entirety. Some White People's views of our group are informed only by what they hear or see from a few People of Color acting from the early orange section; for example, exploding into violence or horizontal violence. Either way, White culture continues as the valued culture and the right way to be in the world. We aspire to White culture instead of our home cultures, thus reinforcing White People's belief that their way of life is the only one that really counts. Much of the orange section is about how we collude, often unconsciously, with White People, to maintain this fiction.

The profound negation of Peoples and Cultures of Color forces us to **manipulate** circumstances to keep White People comfortable. We go out of our way to maintain their comfort because our survival depends on it. We are particularly anxious to minimize White People's discomfort around matters of race. We perform a kind of social engineering, using strategies such as redirecting the conversation, placating other People of Color, smoothing emotions, and excusing, explaining, and swallowing racially offensive remarks and events to manipulate social space for White People's comfort.

Keeping White People comfortable is such a high priority for us that it pervades much of the diversity training being done in organizations. Despite the "be open and honest" guideline, we downplay or withhold certain truths of our experience. Many training programs encourage participants to value multiculturalism and "all the diversities" so as to avoid uncomfortable truths about institutional and structural racism and to maintain equilibrium for White People, especially those in role authority. This dynamic is also evident in advertising, politics, and in other aspects of social life.

We are forced to **endure** the micro-aggressions and macro-aggressions thrown at us every day from being culturally subordinated. Enduring means doing whatever is necessary to survive from one day to the next. To endure is synonymous with what it means to be a Person of Color in White-dominant culture. Strategies include stifling or silencing ourselves, masking our differences, deferring to White People's comfort needs, smiling to cover fear and anxiety, never complaining, taking micro-aggressions in stride, and swallowing our anger and frustration in the presence of White People. These survival strategies create high levels of stress resulting in physical and mental fatigue, loss of health, and finally loss of self. This is true wherever we are on our journey. Enduring alone with no hope of ever being included in the mainstream ultimately leads to disease in the bodies and psyches of People of Color.

People of Color at the Midpoint of the Orange Section

Struggle for respect emerges in the middle of the orange section. We struggle in small ways to regain and maintain our dignity, pushing out our chest with pride in the face of adversity. We emulate White People's manner of self-presentation in our dress, hair styles, and speech as a way to ask for respect. When it feels like something is missing from our cultural experience, we try to compensate with material possessions.

Education is enormously important to us as a lever for social mobility, out of subordinated race status. We lead with our credentials rather than with knowledge and expertise. When we achieve a doctorate in any field, we use that credential when introducing ourselves, so it's as if "Doctor" becomes our first name.

When about to enter a mixed-race situation, we are cautious about whether to express ourselves fully for fear of making White People uncomfortable enough to judge us. We deny ourselves the privilege of authentic self-expression. In a similar vein, African American parents are anxious for their children's behavior to be above reproach, given the "ghetto" stereotype of their children. Playful by nature, they can be seen as out of control by any White People present.

Internalized oppression is endemic to the subordinated group in Cultural Dominance & Subordination. A phenomenon that exists only when those system dynamics are in place, it manifests when a subordinated group absorbs the dominant group's negative attitudes and stereotypes, allowing dominant group views to define its reality and self-image (how they see themselves and others in their group).

Once we internalize racism, it makes us see our lives, our culture, and each other as having less value than White People's lives and culture. When internalized oppression is juxtaposed with a sense of an authentic self, it creates a great deal of tension. We relieve the tension by identifying with White-dominant culture and differentiating and distancing ourselves from anything having to do with our own communities, cultures, or histories.

The costs associated with internalized oppression are high. First, subordinated status debases the things that are most authentically part of our racial-cultural heritage and identity. Internalized oppression damages our self-image and sense of self-worth.

Second, internalized oppression contributes to horizontal violence among and between People of Color because of the social phenomenon of mirroring. It works like this: *When I look at you, if you look like me, I see someone whose life has less value than the lives of White People, so I think your life should be snuffed out. When I lash out at you, I am really lashing out at myself. I see myself reflected in the mirror of your being, so I despise you as I despise myself, enough to want to hurt you or wipe you out.*

For example, African Americans disassociate themselves from anything that suggests African American or African culture; Japanese Americans silence themselves about their incarceration in U.S. concentration camps; Asian Americans are silent about how recent their admission into citizenship was; Latino Americans devalue their language by abandoning it; American Indians try to blend in with their White heritage if they are not full-blood. We accept one-dimensional, stereotypical, White notions and interpretations of our history. We gaze on a "White" appearance (lighter skin, large eyes) and White lives as ideal, and get excited about White cultural icons.

Our psychological vulnerability is so great in moments like this that we blindly accept the system, trying to draw attention away from our difference. We are relieved and glad just to be surviving. Our default belief is that this is the way it has always been, and it is never going to change. This belief is so ingrained in us that we uncritically accept a system that sees us as an inferior part of it, and requires us to lose more of our authentic selves to be granted even marginal inclusion.

Shame about our **history** is deeply embedded in us once we have internalized the oppression. Our ancestry and cultural heritage embarrasses us, not so much for being old-fashioned but for being out of step with the mainstream (popularly accepted) version of Western history. It is humiliating to realize that in the past, our people were viewed by White People as so uncivilized that they deserved to be brutalized or exterminated. It is shameful to contemplate the historical fact that we were subjected to genocide, slavery, U.S. concentration (internment) camps, forced labor, relocation camps, reservations, BIA* schools, ghettos and "projects".

Understandably, many of us choose not to identify with the shameful and painful aspects of our history. It may have happened to our ancestors, but we want to believe that it doesn't affect our lives in the present day. We do all we can to disassociate ourselves from the past of our people. It is impossible for us, at this stage in our journey, to comprehend the pride that others in our racial identity group feel for our home culture. We have bought into distortions of our group and its history that were socially constructed by White People.

---

* Bureau of Indian Affairs

We don't like who we are, so we unconsciously **fantasize about being White**; that is, being (and *being seen as*) a good and worthy person, valued in society. Whiteness is the standard by which we judge ourselves. We idealize various expressions of White culture and identify ourselves with them, leading us to seek honorary White status by emulating White communication styles (e.g. manners of speech, vocal patterns, rhythms, tones, and modulation); White styles of working, managing, and leading; and frequenting White restaurants and places of entertainment. We gratefully accept the pseudo-compliment when a White person says, "You're not like those other _____." There is an enormous associated cost, however, when a Person of Color individualizes him- or herself to seek or accept honorary White status because it perpetuates the subordinated status of the whole group.

In **unquestioning acceptance of the system,** we literally do not notice the oppression and inequities embedded in Cultural Dominance & Subordination. It has been this way for so long that we assume it is never going to change. Feeling hopeless, we do not even see and certainly do not challenge unfair policies or practices that perpetuate our subordinated status. Our vulnerability at this point on the journey lies in the fear that if we share parts of ourselves with White People that we have kept hidden from them up until now, they will not believe us, or will misunderstand or reject us, or use what we disclose to harm us. We resist opening ourselves up because the need to be guarded remains high. We are still in a place of **distrust**.

However, we are having an inner dialogue about whether the current circumstances might justify saying something more about ourselves than we ordinarily would. Our guardedness is less automatic. We make conscious choices about whether to open up and share our thoughts and feelings, based on an assessment of the current context, including the White person sitting across from us.

Still, we resist having our authentic selves found out. It continues to be important to maintain the charade of being different from other People of Color (if not White). We are still reacting to previous boundary violations or other harms inflicted by unaware White persons. Our struggle is focused now on questions such as Who am I? Where did I come from? What is the image I want to present? How do I do myself now?

It is impossible for us to realistically assess ourselves or see how others perceive us because the White-dominant world we live in, which is not real for us, isolates us from our home culture. White culture norms and practices require us to **survive by projecting** and **stereotyping**. We watch how White folk interact with each other and with us, then interpret their behavior *without being able to check our interpretations for accuracy.* Dominant-and-subordinated group system dynamics prohibit us from checking our assumptions with the people that we have them about.

White People are unsafe for us until we come to know some of them as individuals. We prepare ourselves for an encounter with a White person by projecting to stay safe. Failing to do so is likely to cause regret after the fact. We continuously watch White People for behavior that supports our assumptions and reinforces our projections. This applies across the board to all White People, *until trust is earned by each of them.* Our extreme vulnerability forces us to be highly selective about our interactions.

Talking about racial inequality across race difference is just not done at any point in the orange section, so the way we deal with White People is governed by the stereotypes we have of them, as a group. We treat them indiscriminately, as if they are all the same. We have little-to-no experiential knowledge that would give us meaningful data on the differences among them. If one White person treats us or reacts to us in a certain way, we expect that all the others will do the same. Actual, lived experience with White People has taught us that our expectations do play out in reality. This awareness is always in the forefront of our consciousness in an encounter with any White person.

If we do not interact with White People very often, we protect ourselves to be safe. In mixed-race groups in the workplace, on sports teams, or in the entertainment world, we are **self-protective,** with conscious and deliberate strategies. If a White person behaves in a threatening or confusing way, it is easier to withdraw and close our boundary if we start from a self-protective stance. We always size up a situation for safety, wondering when we can be more open. In the late orange section, we long to live beyond only fight-or-flight ways of being in the world. We yearn to experience more thoughtful and less reactive ways of responding to or engaging with others.

The collective silence we maintain about our common experience as members of a culturally subordinated group damages all of us, as with many Japanese Americans who have kept silent about the trauma from being "interned" in U.S. concentration camps during World War II. Many persons delayed processing that trauma for many years, while others never will, having taken their trauma to the grave.

People of Color in the Late Orange Section

In an effort to be more thoughtful in the late orange section, we begin to share our experiences in affinity groups: Arab Americans with other Arab Americans; Asian Americans with other Asian Americans; Latinos/as with other Latino/as; African Americans with other African Americans; American Indians with other American Indians; and so on. **Processing within identity groups** allows us to talk about the humiliation and indignities that we are subjected to by White People and the emotions we are left with. The group is safe enough to ask "Am I crazy? Have you ever experienced this?" trusting that support and honest feedback will be there.

Affinity groups are a safe haven and a respite from being in largely White social contexts where we must push ourselves to be **over-competent** and over-nice in hopes that White People will accept us – again, so we can survive. In the safe haven of my affinity group, my guard can be down and I do not have to speak in a prescribed way.

Given how minimal and infrequent our interactions with White People are, we can be hyper-reactive when we do encounter them and their ways. When our experience in the orange section has been too painful, too frustrating, or too exhausting, we fantasize about reversing the power paradigm and sometimes do **reverse dominance** on a White person to show them how it feels. We might explode into intimidating behavior with White People to put them in *their* place, allowing ourselves to feel, for a moment, that we have subordinated White People *to us*. We do this with the intention to overwhelm and intimidate. As is the case with all our orange-section behavior, however, *we are only reacting*, not being proactive or assertive on our own behalf.

At this point, the pain and frustration of life in the orange section have become intolerable, forcing us to experiment with other ways of being and behaving. It is in this moment that we **shift** our **identity from victim to survivor.** No longer trying merely to survive, we are **seeking to thrive.** We say "Enough!" to suffering, second-class status, and being less-than. We begin to take pride in our identity as survivors. We shift the onus for our situation off ourselves and onto the system, empowering ourselves to take action on our own behalf.

We **test for what can be shared with White People,** finding a few who seem to care about their behavior and its impact, and are not so focused on controlling us. We might hear about an experience from someone in our support network that sounds different from what we are used to experiencing from you (White People).

I experiment by saying something to see what your reaction is. I might share something insignificant about myself or my family to see how you react or respond. I am testing for how natural and authentic I can be in your presence. Inside I am wondering whether you are *able* to stay with me and my experience. Even more importantly, will you *choose* to stay with me and my experience … are you *capable* of staying with me and my experience or will you go right back to the centrality of Whiteness? Now, in the last stage of the orange section, we are numbing ourselves less as we move toward the Transition.

People of Color in the Transition (Blue Section)

The core task for us as People of Color in the Transition is to **differentiate** our **identity from subordinated group status,** a necessary first step before we can actualize ourselves to our full potential. We work to reclaim and re-empower ourselves and our communities from the scourge of subjugation to restore the fullness of our humanity. The first-person voice, both singular and plural, is used to represent both the individual and the community. The author is a Person of Color*.

WE DECIDE TO CHANGE FOR THE SIMPLE REASON THAT LIFE IN THE ORANGE SECTION IS JUST TOO PAINFUL.

People of Color in the Early Transition

Moving into the Transition is challenging for us. As we work to differentiate our identity from subordinated group status, we ask ourselves hard questions about our lives in White-dominant culture: Who am I, really? Who do I want to be? How can I manage myself differently around my anger, depression, and vulnerability?

It is very important to make **constructive use of** our **anger** now. We are painfully aware that White

* Rick Huntley

Men's anger is tolerated in White-dominant culture while anger expressed by People of Color, especially African American men and Latinos, is met with the severest sanctions, not even the merest shred of tolerance. We must be extremely vigilant around our anger and how we express it, if at all.

African Americans especially are sensitive to the White-culture stereotypes of the Angry Black Man and Angry Black Woman. If we should ever express our anger openly and forthrightly, we are quickly made aware that doing so is not to our advantage. At that point we are seen only for our anger, instead of being seen as a whole person with emotional range and a rich, expansive inner life that is worth getting to know.

In the Transition, we become more interpersonally effective by experiencing and expressing emotions other than anger. We do not judge ourselves for feeling angry when treated unjustly, but we want to avoid acting out anger in ways that harm others. Yelling, cursing, or hitting are to be avoided. We want to honor the emotion but behave appropriately for the social context.

Anger is justified in certain situations, and there are constructive ways to express it. We examine how and when we expressed anger in the past, and what the impact was so we can learn from the experience. We learn new language for expressing ourselves and bring new behaviors to interactions that communicate our reality constructively so that others can hear it. Over time we learn to differentiate between anger-the-emotion and angry behavior. We realize that we have options and can make choices about how to act, almost irrespective of what we feel. Our ability to self-manage in this manner makes it less likely that others will see us in such simplistic terms as before. We are not our anger, nor are we controlled by it.

Early in the Transition, we may decide to tell White People about the impact of their resistance to change on us. This is a big first step toward sharing our thoughts and feelings directly and constructively with White People themselves instead of only talking about it among ourselves. We are taking a big risk because we are fresh out of the orange section where collusion is the unwritten social-psychological contract between us and White People at the intergroup level.

Although it is not easy for us to let go of feeling responsible for White People's discomfort, it is essential for us to do so. They need to feel their emotions without us making things easy for them. It is essential for our individual and collective well-being that we do let go, however difficult that might be. A White person may want to talk to us about how bad they are feeling, whether hurt, sad, angry, guilty, or ashamed, with the expectation that because they are sharing and being honest, we will make them feel better (i.c. restore their comfort and equilibrium).

Until now, we have not known how to engage in a conversation like this, nor has it been a priority. Survival was paramount. We were forced to use all available energy to protect ourselves from White People's violence and projections onto us. We need to realize that the hurt, anger, and emerging shame that come over White People as they struggle to move out of the orange section and into their own Transition are probably a reaction to us an our own mid-Transition behavior. *We need to stay with ourselves, stand in our own experience, and let them stand in theirs.* We can listen to them share and even appreciate their honesty and their struggle, *but we need to let them have their struggle and not take it on as our own.* We need to allow them to be comfortable and not try to fix them.

We **decide to change** for the simple reason that life in the orange section is just too painful. Being subordinated has brought everything we do not want and nothing we do want. We begin to realize the importance of claiming our race-color-ethnic identity with pride: I am a Chicana; I am Japanese; **I'm Black, I'm proud**; I am Sudanese; I am an Arab person. We realize that claiming identity is not enough, however, and so acknowledge the need to change how we think and act in the world.

In our affinity and support groups, we explore our heritage and the contributions our groups have made to U.S. history and culture. We begin to take pride in our ancestries and heritage. We realize that our cultures are different from White-dominant culture and that there is a lot to be proud of. We leave shame behind.

All the dimensions of culture contribute to the unique makeup of each of us: our style, how we live, our way of being in the world. When I can bring my cultural differences into a relationship with a White person, it allows me to bring the authenticity of my being and the integrity of my wholeness. My biculturalism helps me do that. It also encourages my interest in and appreciation for other Cultures of Color as well as culturally subordinated groups other than my own.

In the early Transition, we are still dealing with the aftermath of being subordinated. We sometimes find ourselves back in the orange section, perhaps with little understanding of how we got there. Sometimes we put ourselves there on purpose for safety. However, there is less unconscious pre-Transition behavior in this part of the journey. For example, with White People who are in charge and acting out White cultural dominance in conjunction with their formal role power, we might go back to testing what can be shared with them because our job feels at risk.

Our task now is to **undo** our **subordinated status.** A complicated set of tasks is involved in this location on the Continuum. We spend more time in identity or affinity groups to work through these tasks. Being subordinated was a way of life that must now be examined with a critical eye. To undo it, we need to see the reality of internalized oppression and deal continuously with its effects on us.

Colorism among and between People of Color mimics the racial hierarchy invented by White People*. It is one of the ways we have of oppressing each other. The essence of colorism is a concern about physical appearance. Under the harsh

---

* The racial hierarchy is discussed in Chapter 1.

light of White standards of beauty, we examine ourselves and each other for whose appearance is closer to the White ideal, buying in to the notion that the whiter you look, the more beautiful you are. We practice colorism when we assess someone's skin color (lighter is better), eye size and shape (bigger and rounder is better), and hair color and texture (straight and shiny better; blonde is best). Persons with the darkest color suffer the most because the darkest skin colors are at the bottom of the colorism hierarchy.

Despite how deeply damaging it is to self-esteem, colorism is rife in People of Color communities. At this stage of our journey, the work is to notice colorism, undo it in ourselves, and speak out against it in our groups and communities. We need to create a safe container together to support our healing and self-development work as we discuss colorism among ourselves. It's important to be non-judgmental as we explore this sensitive topic. The less we judge ourselves and each other, the safer the container will be, and the safer the container is, the deeper our work can go and the greater the healing will be.

Competition *within* identity groups is another manifestation of internalized oppression. Being subordinated forces us to compete with one another for acceptance and approval from White People and thus, for access to the resources they control. It was central to our lives in the orange section but now it is important to notice competition among us in the Transition: to see how it hurts us, and work to undo it.

Competition *between* different People of Color identity groups is also common. All People of Color strive against each other for acceptance, recognition, and approval in a White-dominant world. We assess each other, within and between identity groups, in terms of class, education level, language, and skin color. Who looks and acts more White? The Transition asks us to look at intra- and inter-group competition dynamics: How ingrained are they in our behavior and worldviews? How do they impact us?

The need to always know: So much is required of us simply to survive in the orange section that we are chronically tense with worry. We worry about what we might not know and about looking bad. Concerned with proving ourselves, we have a strong need to be acknowledged for who we are and what we can do. This need pushes us to be over-competent and always knowledgeable. What is emerging now in the Transition is a release from the burden of always needing to know.

Being okay with not knowing allows us to build on others' ideas at the same time as we bring what we do know into the discussion. In this way, we begin to value other differences that may not be visible (e.g. an ability issue, religion, gender identity), a process that can happen only when there is a high degree of trust in the group. It is virtually impossible to seek or accept information from others whom we do not trust.

A final aspect of dealing with the effects of subordinated status is that we **begin to live** more **authentically** now. Being more comfortable with our authentic selves means that we do not need to fabricate reality or camouflage ourselves any longer. We are willing to present ourselves more fully and honestly. Our concern for White People's comfort lessens as our authenticity grows and we have more pride in our cultures – the truths of our lives.

Living more authentically **calls forth** our **personal power** and enables us to **connect** more deeply **with other People of Color.** Taking the initiative and generating ideas at work, sharing experiences and insights that are different from dominant culture norms, leveraging resources to position ourselves for equitable treatment: all are now means available to us that call forth our personal power. Comfortable with our differences now, we refuse to allow others' reactions to our skin color, immigrant status, language or accents to diminish our contributions.

We become psychologically and emotionally acclimated to social space in the Transition as we move further into it, developing a sense of how our differences and biculturalism are sources of strength. We experiment with integrating our racial identity with other parts of ourselves - our intellect, language, and spirit. As all the aspects of our identity are woven into an integral whole, we can bring a more robust self to our families, friendships, communities, work life, and creative projects.

Our empowerment makes us more visible to White People. They are literally seeing us for who we are now, along with the differences among us, and between us and them. How they experience and react or respond to our differences depends on where they are in their own journeys.

We continue to encounter White People in the orange section who are acting out dominance, whether consciously/intentionally or not. We need to be thoughtful about how to respond in such situations. Every encounter with a White person who is acting out dominance forces us to revisit decide-to-change on the Continuum. Do we defer to dominance, as we were accustomed to doing in the orange section, or do we remain steadfast in our commitment to our own emerging authenticity and empowerment?

It is important to acknowledge the risks involved in changing how we behave. If I act in more empowered ways, are White People going to punish me with exclusion, avoidance, anger, or physical violence? We are moving away from always *re*acting to White People and White culture, and toward being more assertive and *pro*active. We need to empower ourselves because the collective power of our groups and communities grows as each of us steps into and claims our personal power.

People of Color at the Midpoint of the Transition

Being involved in our support and identity/affinity groups and communities **develop**s our **self-esteem***. Such groups are critical to our well-being because they provide a safe place to share experiences and emotions, especially after yet another encounter with a White person acting out White dominance. We can trust colleagues and friends of color with our vulnerability when Whiteness lands on us again.

---

* Some White People do not understand why support/affinity groups for People of Color-only are so necessary for us at this point in our development. However, it is critically important for us to stand for ourselves and our own needs here and not defer to White People's needs for comfort or inclusion.

If we don't nurture these associations with other People of Color, we lose sight of what is needed to sustain community. Interfacing regularly with White-dominant culture at work and in other activities keeps us focused on what is important for and with White People but not for and with ourselves, so it is important to participate in activities that affirm our culture to support and honor the fullness of our humanity.

In African American and Latin cultures, the church nurtures people and builds self-esteem. Historically, when African Americans were denied opportunities in the workplace, the church built up our sense of self-worth by affirming the leadership we provided for our communities and institutions to thrive. Connecting with others like us in the workplace and other institutions, especially where People of Color are not well represented, grounds us and fosters our sense of self-worth.

We each need to **forgive** our **self for doing what was needed to survive.** Healing ourselves and each other from the injuries that come from being subordinated requires forgiveness. We need to remind ourselves that while subordinated group status was/is done *to* us, we do not need to identify with it any longer.

In our communities, we share resources and support each other through the Transition as we move toward the green section. At the same time, the environments we live and work in continue to require the survival strategies we've used throughout our lives. Even as we learn new behaviors and strategies, we can only release the old ones very slowly because we keep running into White People who are still acting out White cultural dominance. It helps when we find White People who have left the orange section behind and are doing their own work in the Transition.

Once I feel proud of my cultural identity, I become **willing to share more** with people outside my identity group. I may be **open to sharing more information about** my**self** in ways that I have long kept hidden. No longer ashamed of my history, I do not ask for permission to share myself if that is what I decide to do.

The Transition brings responsibility as well as freedom, meaning that I am now **willing to own my projections.** What have I been projecting onto White People or other People of Color that is inappropriate or inaccurate? Do I project dominant White stereotypes onto all White People? I have a lot of anger about the dominant behaviors I've been subjected to from many White People, but am I justified in directing that anger onto the White Person I am dealing with right here and now?

My willingness to **individualize White People** is increasing. I take into account where each White person is on their journey out of cultural dominance while assessing their need to subordinate People of Color. I check out their intentions now; I don't just assume that they are rooted in the orange section. If their behavior makes it obvious that they are coming from the orange section, I have the skills at this point to manage myself appropriately around their impact on me. The good news is that differentiating among White People is increasing the number of race allies in my acquaintance.

We are also differentiating more within our communities. We may once have judged other People of Color for not joining us in the Transition. While we understand that in the past it was necessary for our communities to be extremely protective of us if we were to survive, at this point we question whether it is still helpful for the community to be so protective. We realize that in certain contexts, the community is *too* protective. Thus, as an individual I now **differentiate** myself **from** the **over-protectiveness of** the **community.** I also realize that other People of Color may need to be challenged to develop themselves as well as the community.

We have come to realize that each of us must take responsibility for our own journey, if progress is to be made toward Equity & Inclusion in the workplace and community. We all need to take responsibility for ourselves, including the impact of our behavior, and not hide under the cover of the community as if expecting it to shield us no matter what we do. At the same time, we remember that each of us only moves forward on our journey to the extent that we feel safe and supported enough.

People of Color Toward the End of the Transition

When People of Color resist oppression by deciding to change and step over the threshold out of the orange section and into the Transition, backlash is to be expected. Backlash is a strong adverse reaction to a social or political development, and our movement into the Transition is exactly that: a social and political development. It signifies that our social and political power has increased.

We expect backlash from White People, of course (especially from those still living from the White-dominant worldview), but sometimes we also need to **deal with backlash from other People of Color** who are still **in** the **orange section.** They may punish us for individualizing White People such that we no longer see all of them as the oppressor, or accuse us of "acting White" because we work hard to succeed in school or in the corporate world. They may despise and derogate our friendships with White People.

Such People of Color are acting out of the orange section on the Continuum. They do not yet think of themselves as being on a journey out of subordinated group identity or status, *or they have not yet made enough movement on their journeys to view our behavior in the later stage of the Transition as inclusive. They see us as selling out in ways that exclude them, leave them behind*

How do we remain true to our own journey while encouraging others to move forward on theirs without coming across as judgmental or exclusionary? This is our challenge, and it is as necessary as it is painful. Backlash from other People of Color is one of the things we talk about in our affinity or identity support groups.

The Search for Identity

Our **inward journey** is **expanding** as we differentiate our identity from subordinated group status and leave internalized oppression behind. This is the other part of our core task in the Transition. I question myself as I search for a racial-ethnic identity independent of subordinated status, accounting for what I think and how I feel as I define and claim myself as an African American, American Indian, Arab American, Chinese American, Japanese American, Latino/a, Laotian American, Mexican American, Senegalese American and so on, bringing myself fully into a sense of the richness of my identity. I see how my race-color-ethnicity and other aspects of my identity are woven into an integral whole that represents who I am, and I learn more about whatever I do not yet know about my heritage and origins.

We are aware of having lived a bicultural existence out of necessity in Cultural Dominance & Subordination/Racial Inequality. Now we celebrate our biculturalism as a source of strength. Whereas our native language was once seen as a liability, we now see our bilingualism as an asset in the Transition. Many of us are even multicultural and multilingual as we move around in and flex between our culture of origin and others that are less familiar, strengths that are true assets in the global village.

Still Vulnerable

Despite all the work we do in the Transition, we must still be guarded because our **physical & psycho-emotional vulnerability** persist and **increase with unaware White People.** Our comfort with ourselves and the ease with which we participate in social settings such as the workplace can trigger the worst fears, biases, and reactions in orange-section White People. Our empowerment can trigger them into feeling out of control and powerless, and put them in a place where they feel they must act in some way to reestablish control and equilibrium. To sustain ourselves in the Transition and beyond, we need support from White People already living in the Transition. Also, we need to support other People of Color experiencing backlash from orange-section White People, just as we need support from them when it's happening to us.

CHAPTER SIX

White People in the Transition (Blue Section)

The nature of the journey is changing as I approach the Transition. I'm bringing with me the knowledge I gained from my passage through the orange section about the system of Cultural Dominance & Subordination: It exists. It has real impacts on real people's lives. We (White People) created the system and perpetuate it for our own benefit. Now I position myself to focus on learning. I connect with other White People to find support for talking about the taboo topics of race, color, and racism. I do this for my own learning and to change myself, not them.

...DECIDING TO LEARN DRAWS ME INTO DEEPLY EMOTIONAL TERRITORY.

The Transition brings many changes in my relationships with other White People, as well as with People of Color. I may need to examine ties with family and friends who live in the orange section. It's difficult to be patient with them. The farther I move into the Transition, the harder it gets. At the same time, my relationships with People of Color become more significant and meaningful.

The voice in this chapter is different from the voice in Chapter 3, which uses the first-person *plural* to model the collective voice of White People in cultural dominance. Chapter 6 mostly uses the first-person singular to model the voice of the individual taking responsibility for my own personal journey. The authors are White People*.

Democratic Principles and Values

My learning journey matters on a large scale because American democracy is reinvigorated when my behavior creates equity and is inclusive. Our democracy values civil liberties, a government of laws, consent of the governed, and the protection of individual rights from arbitrary authority. Freedom is not only about my rights but also my responsibilities for the common good. The actions of ordinary Americans like me bring the values to life.

White People, as a group, are more protected from arbitrary authority than People of Color. This offends my sense of justice. I want to understand the system and my role in it. How did the socialization practices I was raised with inculcate racism in me? How does my behavior perpetuate racism? How do I undo it in myself? **Doing the work** in the Transition will strengthen the character traits I need to undo racism in me and in my spheres of influence.

White People in the Early Transition

I am dragged into the Transition by a Person of Color who is important to me – a friend, family member, or co-worker – who is already into their own Transition. People of Color are excited about the Transition because it promises greater freedom and new beginnings, but it makes me uncomfortable so I am dragging my heels.

My colleague or friend wants to change the unwritten social contract between us. They don't want to teach, rescue or make excuses for me anymore. They want me to

* Carol Pierce, Rianna Moore, and David Wagner.

take responsibility for myself. I can't believe I am being challenged like this. I don't like to be pushed! **Resistance** and **anger** push up inside. Do I want to learn about the impact of my behavior? Not so much. I feel **hurt** and misunderstood: "I was only trying to help!" "I thought I was *supposed* to be colorblind!"

It feels like the world has been turned upside down, like I'm turned inside out. I am overwhelmed by **confusion**; I'm **frozen; shame** is emerging. On the **defensive**, I plead: **"Look at all I've done!"** If a Person of Color says that something I said or did was racist, I cry, **"I didn't mean to be racist!"** I accuse them of being hypersensitive, playing the race card, or not being able to take a joke.

This is new emotional territory. It's hard to deal with relationships across race difference in this new social space and overwhelming to realize that I have benefited from White cultural dominance and White privilege. It is too painful to dwell on what my racial identity group – my people – have done to People of Color, so I individualize and **credentialize** myself: **"Some of my best friends are…."** I point to my good works and the People of Color who go to my church or my children's school.

I want People of Color to like me. I'm relieved when they individualize me by saying I am different from other White People. I try to be a good person: I do not harbor ill will toward anyone, I don't want to hurt anyone, and I don't understand why others laugh when I wonder why we all can't all get along*. I try to hide my ignorance and inadequacies because the thought of revealing them terrifies me. I think about retreating into the orange section to hide … or retaliate! Then I realize that I can't un-know all that I have learned, and frankly, I don't want to be part of the backlash against People of Color that I see all around me.

---

* "Can we all get along?" is a quote from Rodney King (1965-2012), an African American taxi driver who was savagely beaten by four LAPD officers following a high-speed chase. This event, which took place in 1991, was filmed by an onlooker and broadcast to the nation.

People say that impact matters more than intentions. It's not enough to have good intentions. I've gotten pressure from the job – feedback, too. They want me to be more thoughtful about the effect I want to create, and then align my behavior with that. If I turn away feedback from People of Color, they feel me acting dominant because I am not allowing them to influence me. They don't know how afraid I am. My discomfort grows as the delta widens between my good-person self-image and the feedback I'm getting. Finally, I realize that my choice is to either stay stuck in the pain of resistance, defensiveness, and confusion or "get with the program" and deal with whatever pain that might bring. I step into the Transition when I **acknowledge** the **need to change.**

The journey through the Transition looms. Inner tension grows as I become more aware of the relative safety and comfort of my life in contrast with how challenging, even dangerous daily life can be for People of Color. Teetering back and forth, I look back at who I've been and ahead at what I need to learn.

Decide to learn is key for moving fully into the Transition. It sounds like only a cognitive act, but the fact is that deciding to learn draws me into deeply emotional territory. It pushes me to reflect on painful episodes that I have brought on myself, on my desire to do the right thing, on the support given by White friends and colleagues, and on the grace given by the People of Color in my life who over and over extend themselves on my behalf. Taken together, such reflections make me feel quite tender. They tip the balance so that suddenly I am motivated to learn.

Deciding to learn dissolves my assumption that everything is fine where race is concerned. It frees me to focus on what is actually happening, not on what I assume, hope, or pretend is happening. I'm different here from how I was at the beginning of my journey. Back then, it totally blew my emotional circuitry if someone called me a racist. Now I am less reactive and defensive. I try to hear others' feedback, even their judgments, as "data". If it's just data, I can ask questions and learn from it.

It would be easier if People of Color would just tell me what to do (or not do), but they are angry from having explained racism to White People over and over for years while it seems to never have made a difference. Racism is pervasive in their lives and it's just wrong to expect them to keep explaining it to me. For one thing, that's just one more way of expecting them to take care of me. Also, there's a lot that I already know so to act as if I don't is either disingenuous, willful ignorance, or irresponsible.

I connect with other White people to end the silence, talking about racism, Whiteness, White privilege, White identity, and so on, so we can stop colluding and understand more. The more self-awareness I have, the better I can manage my resistance and defensiveness, the easier it gets to own up to not understanding some things, and the more exciting it becomes to learn and grow.

I work at becoming **willing to look at** my use of **language and projections.** My speech broadcasts my unconscious beliefs and stereotypes about People of Color.

Broadcasting My Derogatory Beliefs & Stereotypes About People of Color: Questions for Self-Examination

- Do I use "black" or "dark" to denote negativity?
- Do I use demeaning, disrespectful, or derogatory terms for People of Color?
- Do I attribute hostile intent to an African American boy or man in a hoodie?
- Do I use labels that may have been acceptable or considered polite at one time but are now disavowed by People of Color?
- Do I stereotype People of Color?

Do I blame People of Color for their subordinated status or do I consider how systemic or structural issues have affected their life chances?

Blaming the Victim	**Acknowledging the Impact of Structural Issues**
They will never have real power or be leaders until they pull themselves up by their bootstraps and stop playing the race card.	There will only be token People of Color in organizational role power as long as structural inequality and institutional racism prevail.

Do I perpetuate racist myths or describe events accurately? I've always believed that People of Color are the perpetrators of race riots and White People the victims but in historical fact, there were many instances* in which mobs of White People terrorized African Americans and destroyed entire African American towns and communities.

Do I use the universal "we" when I'm only talking about White People, or the passive voice to mask the involvement of White People so as to avoid accountability?

Universal We	**Accurate***
Just as many German people tried to wipe out the memory of the Holocaust after WWII, so have we in the US wanted to sweep slavery, the genocide of American Indians, and the internment of Japanese Americans during WWII under the rug.	Just as many German people wanted to wipe out the memory of the Holocaust after WWII, so have White People in the US wanted to sweep slavery, the genocide of American Indians persons, and the internment of Japanese Americans during WWII under the rug.

*African Americans have not forgotten slavery, American Indians have not forgotten the U.S. government's campaign of genocide against them, and Japanese Americans have not forgotten their internment in U.S. concentration camps during WWII.

---

* Christian, C.M. (1999). See pp. 131, 199, 264-265, 285, 311-312, 316-318, 324, 329, 374, and 376.

Universal We	Accurate
It was only recently in U.S. history that we recognized African Americans as fully human.	It was only recently in U.S. history that White People acknowledged the full humanity of African Americans.

Passive Voice, Masking Involvement	Active Voice, Being Accountable
It was only recently in U.S. history that African American people were recognized as fully human.	It was only recently in U.S. history that White People acknowledged the full humanity of African American people*.

* African American persons have always known that they were human.

Do I refer to White People simply as "people" (normal), not mentioning our race, but point to the race of People of Color, making them different/abnormal? To be more equitable, I could either acknowledge my own race or not mention race at all.

White People Are the Norm	More Equitable
Kevin and me were shooting hoops with these Black guys at the Y….	Me and Kevin – two White guys, right? – were shooting hoops with these Black guys Armand, Delvin, and Dwight, at the Y. OR: Five of us were shooting hoops at the Y.
I don't know what the problem is with Anton, the Chilean guy. He won't share during teambuilding and it's getting to be a real problem for everyone else.	What should I do about Anton? He's from Chile and lived there during the Pinochet regime, but he won't open up during teambuilding and it's a sore spot for the rest of us. We're all Americans so maybe there's a cultural thing going on….
This Asian girl in my group can't seem to report the whole story about what her design team is doing, and their reviews aren't as robust as they should be. She needs to get with the program.	I wonder what's going on with this Asian woman in my group. She doesn't talk about her team's achievements. Could the fact that the rest of us are White males have anything to do with her reluctance? I need her to get with the program.

Do I tell racist stories; use slurs, one-liners, or off-hand remarks, then say I was just joking if someone calls me out? Up until recently, racist language and humor in most public discourse had waned. However, it is back with a vengeance in the contemporary moment because of what is being modeled and encouraged by public figures in high places.

I also need to examine my projections*. As long as unconscious orange-section beliefs infect my psyche, I will project derogatory attitudes and emotions onto People of Color. They have always been tuned into the stereotypes, emotions, and judgments I project onto them. They can feel their negative energy as they deal with them every

Projecting onto People of Color		**Owning My Projections**
They make me feel guilty, ashamed, and afraid of doing something wrong. *They make me* feel like I'm walking on eggshells. *They shouldn't do that to me.*		I feel guilty and afraid of doing something wrong. I'm walking on eggshells. Why do I feel this way? What do I need to learn? How can I do myself differently?
She is so angry … I don't dare give her feedback.		I'm afraid of giving her feedback because I'm so angry at her and I feel like she's angry with me. Maybe I need to check that out.
He doesn't do this as well as I do so *he must want me to do it for him but is too embarrassed to ask.*		I think I do this better than him so I'm going to ask if he wants me to do it.
I'll just put some groceries in her cart so *she doesn't have to use all her food stamps.* I won't ask first because *it would be too embarrassing for her.*		I have no idea what her financial situation is so I am not going to assume that she appreciate me putting groceries in her cart.
They are not safe to be around.		I do not feel safe around them.
They wish they were White. They prefer our way of doing things which is why they always copy us.		I have no idea what they think. Maybe I'll ask Tony … he'll tell me what he thinks.

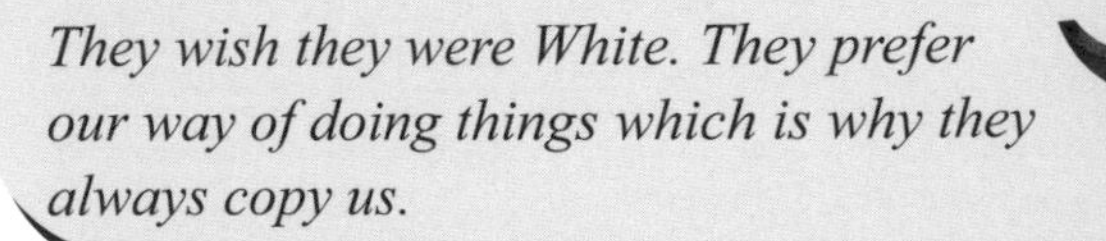

* Described in Chapter 3 on White People in the orange section.

day, even when I try to hide them. I am not to blame for the racism pervading my psyche because it comes from how I was socialized. *However, I am responsible for being aware of and undoing my stereotypical, derogatory projections onto People of Color.* Noticing and taking back my projections is some of the most important work I will do in the Transition.

The best way to calibrate the accuracy of my projections, at least initially, is to check them out in my affinity group. Other White People can help me sort through them. I can also check them out with a Person of Color. However, before I do that, two conditions must be met:

1) I must have a relationship with a Person of Color that feels equitable enough to them*, and

2) My asking needs to be felt by them as respectful, and not as a demand.

Otherwise, my questions are likely to be felt as one more rude, intrusive, arrogant demonstration of White cultural dominance … which is not my intention but is surely going to be my impact. A gossamer thread separates a respectful ask from an intrusive demand, and it is the *receiver* of the question, *not the asker* (me), who discerns between them.

Making assumptions and asking questions outside the context of a relationship perpetuates White dominance because I'm acting as if I am entitled to ask any question of anyone I want to, at any time that suits me. I believe I am special, different from other White People, and expect that the Person of Color across from me sees me that way too. However, all they hear is another clueless White Person insisting on being seen as an individual and not owning my racial identity. They trust me even less when I appear to not know that I'm White.

---

* Remember the inequity in the larger system and at the intergroup-level relationship between our racial identity groups. The energy of these larger-system dynamics is present in any dyadic interaction.

It's frustrating because I am trying to learn and there are things I want to ask about. What to do? One thing is, I can ask other White People who are farther along in their journeys. I can also develop authentic relationships with People of Color that at some point may have the capacity to support an equitable conversation about race.

If I already have a mutually respectful and equitable-enough relationship with a Person of Color (as they assess it, not as I assume it is), I can ask if they are open to a conversation about race. I can explain about being on a learning journey and ask if they would be willing to share their experience. This is one way to create a moment of equity. I do not have the right to assume their willingness or demand self-disclosure. If we get to be comfortable enough together, I won't need to be so cautious because more is being taken for granted between us. But we're not there yet. I'm not there yet.

If my listening conveys respect, White cultural dominance can be undone for a moment. Listening to understand is a different cognitive and emotional process from listening to judge, manipulate, prepare a response, or win. The energy of it feels different. It acknowledges the full personhood of someone whose dignity has suffered from living in culturally subordinated status.

I discover that when I judge myself less harshly, I am less judgmental toward other White People. Our relationship is fragile to begin with from the competition and emotional repression that is the norm in White culture. When I judge you, it damages our relationship because it erodes the trust between us. It makes me unsafe for you. This is important because we need each other's support for a sometimes-painful learning process.

As I **deal with** my **fears**, I realize how self-absorbed I've been. I have not seen the life experiences of People of Color and their cultures as separate and different, only as ancillary to mine. I have never paid attention or entered their culture, so I don't know them as persons, only in terms of their helper and server roles.

I'm disoriented from the challenge to the self-image I've been accustomed to: the White identity I have been unconscious of up until now. I've taken for granted what I now realize is a privileged way of being in the world – an expectation of comfort, a sense of being in charge, a feeling that I should help People of Color, compete with others, and be quick with the answer whether the question was directed to me or not. My normal has meant being in control and central in most social spaces; not allowing People of Color to challenge my ideas and opinions but expecting them to keep me comfortable.

I'm used to dealing with my fears by blocking them out as much as possible. I suppress all emotion, not just fear, especially when a Person of Color is close by. Feeling helpless and out of control makes me freeze so I won't feel anything. About the only thing that still ignites my emotions is being confronted on my racism, but I am becoming more aware now of how I react when this happens.

I notice feeling threatened sooner; for example, when a Person of Color questions an assumption or challenges my authority. Now when this happens, I try to keep from reflexively trying to control the situation or intimidating the other person. My fear needs immediate attention but first I need to notice how disoriented and uncomfortable I am. I try to focus on managing my fear and staying present instead of taking charge or running away. Negotiating my way in dicey moments like these builds my capacity to undo White cultural dominance, in me and out there.

I need to deal with the meanings that People of Color attribute to my Whiteness, much of which is rooted in orange-section dynamics. There are times when all that matters about me to a Person of Color is the color of my skin, no matter what I say or do. That hurts. I feel unseen and unknown. I need to come to grips with the reality that despite all the work I've done on myself, no matter how far I have come on my journey, sometimes all I am to the other person is White. It helps to understand that we are interacting at both intergroup and interpersonal levels of system, simultaneously.

Aware now of my White mono-cultural way of being in the world, I'm appreciating the bicultural strengths of People of Color. They can flex and function in their home culture and in White culture. Some are multicultural because they can flex and function in one another's cultures. I have not had to negotiate another culture in this manner because unfortunately, mainstream culture is organized around the needs of the culturally dominant group, which is backfiring on me now.

My mono-cultural worldview has warped my perceptions of People of Color, like when I assume that subordinated status is the sum and substance of their lives. It does not occur to me that their home cultures hold the most meaning for them. Most People of Color pay no more attention to White culture than needed to get by. They know how to stifle their authentic selves as a matter of personal safety.

When they "act White" to get by, however, they confirm my assumption about their preference for the White way in all things. Once they move into the Transition, they do not tolerate such accommodations or adaptations from themselves or each other so much anymore. They shed the White culture norms, customs, and expectations that do not serve them and press each other to shed them, too. This throws me off balance because my expectations of how we will be with each other in social space are not being met. They are not discomposing themselves to keep me comfortable. They discipline themselves to stop protecting, teaching, rescuing, or taking care of me. I decide to allow myself to be questioned and rethink my beliefs about People of Color.

I am beginning to realize that I pay a price for White supremacy. It pervades my psyche and occludes my self-awareness and sense of what is real, true, and honest. It has led me to believe that I am somehow better than others whose skin is darker than mine. It has kept me from knowing my authentic self, untainted by White-dominant socialization practices, and thus from participating authentically in relationships with others, People of Color and other White People, as well.

White People at the Midpoint of the Transition

The central task for me as a White Person in the Transition is to **undo dominance in** my**self and** in the **system**, but how do I do that? At this point in my journey, it seems like cultural dominance and Whiteness are the same thing, like the Whiteness in the individual and in the culture, are the same. What would be left of Whiteness if cultural dominance were to be taken out of it? I realize that however White I am in terms of my racial identity, I can *act* less typically White by being equitable and inclusive.

The Continuum facilitates learning, supports us as we examine our attitudes and beliefs, and helps us behave differently. I can let go (and encourage other White People to let go) of **control**ling other people and situations. I can be more inclusive. I don't stop being White, but I'm acting less stereotypically White as I model different behavior.

Dominant Group Behavior: Control & Centrality

- I keep others' focus on me – my presence, emotions, ideas, concerns, needs, wishes, and desires – by drawing all the eye contact to myself and taking up a lot of space with large gestures, expansive postures, humor, and other body language.
- I protect the centrality of other White People by responding to them, building on what they say, and co-opting contributions from People of Color, attributing them to a White Person later and giving the White Person the recognition.
- I use forceful body language: holding someone by the arms in a firm grip and speaking forcefully as I look them in the eye; putting my hands on someone's shoulders, literally holding them down; holding my index finger in someone's face.
- I pitch my voice so low that others are forced to lean in to hear me.
- I use dominant postures and stances; for example, standing while others sit, taking the chair at the head of the table, or going into the center of the room and holding that space.
- I take up most or all of the air time.
- I cry to deflect anger or feedback.

Centrality is a key aspect of White cultural dominance. It is a birthright for being White, and whether I'm aware of it or not, I have leveraged it to get to the top. Whatever the top is for me (and whether I get there or not), I tell myself that being there is my due for working hard. I don't even consider how White privilege has helped me get there.

Pushing others out of the center helps me deal with my disorientation fears and hardens my resistance to too much self-examination. I am competitive with other White People in any social space, including in mixed-race groups, because each of us assumes that being central is our prerogative. Once I'm aware of White centrality, I can increase my self-awareness by asking myself questions such as:

- Do I stay in control to maintain my comfort?
- Do I assume centrality and expect others to defer to me?
- Do I bond with other White People to assure centrality?
- Do I focus others' attention on my need to deal with my racism with so much intense emotion that my centrality in social space persists?

Becoming more aware has helped me to manage my centrality needs and given me more choices for how to be more inclusive, so People of Color are experiencing me differently. The outcome is that they are sharing more openly with me so I have come to **appreciate** the **tenuousness**[*] **of everyday life for People of Color.**

People of Color live with the *threat* of physical violence and the *reality* of psychological and emotional violence *every day.* I realize that just because they are somewhat safer with me because I am taking responsibility for myself and doing the work in the Transition, it does not mean that they are safer in the world. I am getting it in my heart and gut, not just in my head, and it blows me away.

---

* "Tenuousness" captures the ambiguity of not being able to count on anything, having to be on guard all the time, the rules changing but no information shared about that, being ungrounded all the time because you never know what might happen, especially as the context shifts.

Who is left out of the loop and not informed of a meeting? Who is not given eye contact? Whose contribution is ignored, then restated by a White Person who receives recognition for it? Who is struggling to establish their leadership in a senior role? Whose authority is undermined with nitpicky questions while giving a presentation? Who is told an apartment has been rented, a house has been sold, a job has been filled … only to find out later they were lied to? Who is ignored or disrespected in a restaurant? Whose son was shot during a routine traffic stop or while walking home from the store?

I pay more attention, *not to protect or rescue* People of Color but to *notice their experience,* and then ask about how that was for them … *unless they are experiencing a particularly violent form of racism and need intervention on their behalf,* not a question about "how that was for them". At minimum, I want to notice their experience and ask about it later. If I believe I have observed a racist, micro-aggression, I can invite a friend or co-worker to talk about it with an open-ended question (e.g. "How are things going?"), creating space for them to share if they want to but refraining from intruding or demanding. I may notice a micro-aggression or micro-inequity that a Person of Color has not noticed, perhaps when no People of Color are in the room. Noticing what used to escape me is exciting, which can enlarge my sense of self-importance. However, I would be wrong to assume that People of Color are safer in the world because of how I am changing.

Everyday life will be tenuous for People of Color for a long time to come, regardless of what I am learning or how I am doing myself differently. People of Color become *more* vulnerable in the Transition to the physical, psychological, and emotional predations of early orange-section White People who feel threatened by a competent, strong, independent, confident Person of Color and are angry at the political and socioeconomic empowerment of People of Color as a group. I want to distance myself from the White perpetrators of this emotional and psychological violence.

In the Transition, I need to focus on myself, not on "helping" People of Color. I am ready to **acknowledge** my **White group membership** and explore my White identity. I can't learn what I need to if I only associate with groups that espouse White supremacy, White nationalism, and race hatred, or are complacent in their White Liberalism. I convene with other White People who, like me, are committed to this learning journey. It helps to know that I'm not the only one in this boat.

Being in an affinity group over time increases my ability to **tolerate discomfort and ambiguity.** Being able to tolerate discomfort is healthy, mature self-management. When I am uncomfortable with

Affinity Groups Give White People the Opportunity to....

- learn about cultural dominant group & subordinated group system dynamics, White privilege, institutional racism, structural inequality, and so on
- share stories about incidents we witnessed or participated in growing up or in more recent times, and reflect on how we handled ourselves
- talk about current events
- learn and notice more
- talk about the fear, guilt, and shame we have kept hidden up until now; accept feeling disoriented, vulnerable, and unsure of ourselves
- be **open to** receiving **feedback on** our racist behaviors
- work through our confusion about how People of Color are dealing with us and our embarrassment, judgment, anger, and defensiveness
- let go of needing to always be in control, learn how to allow conversation to flow, and not always have the last word
- envision equitable and inclusive social space with People of Color – how to create and be in it
- build courage to acknowledge and deal with White privilege.

emotional intensity, I may feel unsafe, but in fact I am safe, unless actual physical harm is imminent.

However intense my discomfort might be, I can undo a bit of dominance by staying on the discomfort hook to see what emerges. What can I learn or do differently if I lean in rather than expecting to be rescued? Playing the I'm-feeling-unsafe card makes my discomfort a problem for others because a demand to be excused or taken care of is implicit when I play it. A highly functional move I can make when I'm on that discomfort hook is to simply state my truth: "I'm uncomfortable right now". This gives others access to me which, in turn, increases their trust in me. At some point, I am struck by the irony of my feeling unsafe because of some emotional intensity when life is generally so tenuous for People of Color. This deepens my appreciation for how safe and relatively comfortable I've been in my life.

My affinity group encourages me to let go of having to think everything through before saying anything (another way to maintain control). My **emotions** are getting **engaged** so that little by little, I can drop into confusion, uncertainty, and vulnerability without defending myself, withdrawing, or controlling. Experiencing emotions is a normal and necessary part of the journey because it shows me how deep my control needs are and how much I have manipulated people, events, and situations to maintain comfort and control.

Suddenly I am experiencing my emotions as a wholly integral person. I am authentically being with the experience of discomfort in the here-and-now. No one is rescuing me, and I am not escaping by being a smart aleck or withdrawing into myself or a mobile device; nor do I walk out, interrupt, over-talk, or crack jokes.

If People of Color accommodate my control needs, the comfort I feel is an illusion. They are colluding and I am deceiving myself. I need to de-center myself but stay present. If another White person takes up too much air time, I redirect the group's attention. If a Person of Color asserts a different worldview, I stay present and engaged for what I might learn.

White People in the Late Transition

I've done enough work in the Transition to feel more solid at this point, making me even more committed to learning, so I decide to open myself to feedback on the impact of my behavior. Feedback is a primary means of understanding my impact. If I don't know the basics of effective feedback, I learn them now*.

It makes me anxious to imagine being given feedback by anyone, but I owe my most impeccable listening presence to someone who is willing to give it to me. I need to manage my defensiveness and soften my boundary to be open to it. I also need support for dealing with my Inner Critic who is capable of paralyzing and disabling me with fear, guilt, and shame. When that happens, I stop moving forward on my journey because of how unsafe I feel. I need to pay attention to what I'm doing and saying in all social contexts, notice the impacts, reflect on my experience, learn and change from my own observations, and seek and listen to feedback from People of Color as well as other White People.

In the late Transition, I am **increasingly direct & non-protective** toward People of Color so our relationships become more authentic. I am less afraid to ask how they feel or what their experience is, and more willing to share my own vulnerability. They are being quite direct, pushing me to explain myself, and I'm more skilled at giving them feedback. Some of the feedback I'm getting says that my interaction style is hierarchical and competitive. This style is a problem for some White People, albeit congruent with White culture norms. It is even more challenging for People of Color because it reinforces the culturally subordinated status of their group.

Gender difference plays a role here too. White Men use paternalism with People of Color *and* White Women, but White Women control White Men with

---

* Briefly, effective feedback 1) is asked for, 2) describes a specific behavior and its impact, and 3) is about something that the receiver can change. NTL Institute's Human Interaction learning laboratory teaches feedback skills (and other interpersonal skills) and facilitates feedback processes (www.ntl.org).

manipulation and indirectness. People of Color do not respect these strategies. To them, White Women's indirectness and manipulation is domineering, controlling, and cowardly.

I'm becoming more aware of how I have thought of People of Color as a group, essentially depersonalizing them. Now I **individualize People of Color,** appreciating each person's unique biography and mix of social identities, characteristics, gifts, and styles. This capacity lays the groundwork for authentic relationship. I realize that pretending to not see color denies some of the richness that a person can bring to our relationship or the team. Affecting colorblindness and not individualizing People of Color puts me right back in the orange section.

Study has brought me to a **beyond-dominant view of history,** making me rethink the history of civilization I was taught in school. Western culture is given credit for achievements in science, technology, medicine, industry, architecture, religion, education, literature, politics, philosophy, the law, and warfare. The discoveries and contributions of peoples from other cultures, from antiquity to the present, are typically overlooked but many of the accomplishments attributed to White Western culture came from them. This new knowledge mitigates the assumption of superiority of my White Western worldview.

Moving beyond a White-dominant view of history is another step toward being a **race ally** and **deal**ing with **WP in the orange section.** A race ally is an anti-racism change agent who takes racism on, naming it whether People of Color are in the room or not. They document and report racism. They examine policies, procedures, and laws for bias and get them changed. They educate and mentor others to raise awareness and undo racism. The following real-life cases illustrate some skills and strategies used by race allies in different roles.

Situation 1: The engineering team has asked Kearney, the only Person of Color in the group, to describe how People of Color are treated differently in the organization. He has come up with several examples, but other members (all White Men) express doubt and keep insisting that they need more data.

Race Ally Intervention: The White team leader says, "I hear Kearney giving us data, based on his own and other people's experience. It's just a different type of data from what we are used to. He has given us three examples, or data points, already. I'm going to restate one from my notes, then I want to hear one from each of you. Kearney, you listen and tell us if we got it right, then we'll go on from there.

Skills Used by Race Ally/Change Agent:

- acknowledging the credibility of Kearney's data so he feels seen, heard, and valued
- interrupting/confronting others' undermining and sabotage of Kearney; putting them on notice that their behavior is unacceptable and not going unnoticed
- holding others accountable for active listening and doing the work of identifying data points
- doing all of the above in a no-blame, no-shame manner

Situation 2: Similar to above, but Alicia has withdrawn (sitting back, eyes downcast) after the first challenge.

Race Ally Intervention: The White team leader says, "Alicia, I hear you saying that People of Color are treated differently here. What you are saying is important to me. I would like to understand better. If you are willing to say more now, I'd like to take time for that right now; otherwise, I'll put it on the agenda for the next meeting and you and I can talk offline before then. What makes sense to you, Alicia?"

Skills Used by Race Ally/Change Agent:

- reflective listening that conveys respect
- creating space – inviting, not demanding
- appropriate use of self-disclosure
- supporting the agency of the Person of Color
- modeling all of the above for others on the team

Situation 3: A White team member has asked Harold, the lone African American on the team, what the position of "the community" is on an issue.

Race Ally Intervention: Another White member says, "I hear Harold expressing his own opinion, though I would like him to say when he might speak for a wider People of Color community. My guess is that we all have opinions, and I'd like to hear them all. Harold, if you don't mind, I'll start."

Skills Used by Race Ally/Change Agent:

- interrupting expectation that a Person of Color can, will, or should speak for their group
- taking Person of Color off the hot seat that he shouldn't be on to begin with
- expecting Person of Color to have expertise, insights, and perspectives on topics other than race
- leveling the playing field
- modeling effective behavior

Situation 4: Several members of the all-white group are talking about how smokers and overweight people suffer from oppression as much as People of Color do.

Race Ally Intervention: The team leader says, "Say more about how your experience compares to that of a Latino or an American Indian in this part of the country." Or, "My hunch is that we all have an experience of being one-down for some reason. I think it would be useful to share those experiences … I know they are painful. Mine is. At the same time, I wonder if any of these experiences can compare to being one-down from being submerged in institutional racism. Let's talk about the similarities and differences."

Skills Used by Race Ally/Change Agent: Takes the onus for naming what's happening and leading a discussion without People of Color present, using a collegial and supportive tone/approach.

Situation 5: An external audit has pointed out that the organization's policies, procedures, and practices discriminate against People of Color.

Race Ally Intervention: The division VP convenes a change action team to review the findings and create a plan for addressing the issues. She ensures that a cross-section of the organization's membership is represented and all skillsets needed are onboard. She supports organization developmental change initiatives with external experts and makes coaches available to support individual development. She builds accountability measures into the change initiatives. She models and actively leads the change process overall.

Skills Used by Race Ally/Change Agent:

- accepting outside agency's findings and taking initiative to address
- including representation from various identity groups and other stakeholders
- visible presence, modeling, involvement, and sponsorship

As a race ally, my stance is that *I* own the problem: Something is happening that concerns me, and I want it to be addressed. I deal with racism and practice inclusion in my spheres of influence. I focus on doing my own work – White People's work – and leave the work that belongs to People of Color to them. It takes courage to be a race ally because orange-section White People look on us as traitors to the White race and sometimes take action against us.

My activism and race ally stance have become such a part of me that I **lose connections with other White People** who live in the orange section. They might be friends, co-workers, or family members. Trying to describe the changes I'm going through is complicated and they do not want to hear it anyway. They want me to be the way I used to be. I spend less time with people stuck in orange-section denial but am between a rock and a hard place because some of those relationships are important so I try to maintain them despite the splits that have developed between us.

I want to preserve my relationships with certain orange-section White People and call out orange-section behavior. Is it possible to maintain connection *and* be a race ally? Maybe staying in the relationship *is* being a race ally, so long as I do not drop back into the orange section myself. It is an unwieldy paradox in an ambiguous situation, one more challenge that other White People on their own journey can help me with.

If I can be a race ally without alienating the White People whose behavior I may need to deal with at some point, then I have attained a degree of mastery. Racism harms White People too, so being a race ally serves all our best interests, although others may not see it that way. With that mindset in place, I work on not judging, blaming, or shaming other White People while staying connected to them so we can work together.

I am finding Whiteness so abhorrent that I may **over-identify with People of Color:** disavowing my race or forgetting I'm White. I may even decide to *be* a Person of Color. I want to show what I know and make change happen. In my enthusiasm for social change I am hypervigilant sometimes push too hard. Other White People are overwhelmed and alienated from me by my anger and judgment. I compete with them to be the most "anti-racist racist" in the room. Sometimes I speak *for* People of Color as if I am their protector, defender, or champion. My holier-than-thou act has damaged my relationships with White People, so I need to do better at managing my emotions, judgments, and projections. If other White People do not feel safe with me, we won't be able to support each other on our journeys, and I need them with me.

I have become **willing to experience multiple cultures.** In previous experiences in other cultures, I carried Whiteness like a shield against discomfort, expecting White culture norms to be observed because I am in the room. Now I connect with the spirit of another culture. Having a sense of how White culture is different from People of Color cultures helps me do better at being fully present outside White culture.

Differences* between White Culture and People of Color Cultures

Dimensions of Culture	**White-Western Culture**	**People of Color Cultures**
Becoming vs. Being	Becoming: future orientation, concern for acquiring material goods, competitive striving	Being: here-and-now orientation; valuing quality of presence, non-material spirituality, a sense of the whole and being in it together
Relationship to Time	Be *on* time; rigid Future-forward thinking: make progress toward future; continuous improvement	Be *in* time: flexible, contextual. Live fully in the here-and-now with a sense of the present nested in the past; consider effects of decisions on future generations
Relationship to Nature	Use and control nature; separate from nature oneself	Nature regulates itself; identify, cooperate with, and protect nature
Identity	See self as individual, not as group; see People of Color as groups	Identify with own racial group; see White People and other Peoples of Color as groups
Thinking & Decision Making Style	Binary (yes/no, either/or, good/bad, right/wrong, black/white, up/down, etc.) "Hard" data; scientific proof Analysis Cognition only; emotion factored out; work by the book	Holistic-systemic-complex: both/and, paradox, ambiguity Include other types of data, e.g. others' descriptions of lived experience Intuition *and* analysis Cognition; emotion factored in; consider impact on people
Conflict Style	Compete	Cooperate/Compromise/Collaborate or Avoid
Orientation to Content & Process; Relationship	Content task considered first; individual before team, group, or community; relationships form by working on content task	Relationship (team, group, community) and process considered first as a resource for working on content task
Philosophy	Free will; create your own reality; mind over matter	Destiny, fate, God's will

* These differences are expressed as generalities, not stereotypes. Generalities are based on real data and allow exceptions while stereo types are based on very little data and do not allow exceptions.

No aspect of culture is inherently problematic; each is simply experienced and expressed differently from one culture to the next. Similarly, none are inherently dominant or subordinated, only in the context of White supremacy. For example, the *destiny, fate, God's will* philosophy is as valid as any other, but it becomes a tool of oppression when White People turn it against People of Color to blame them for their subordinated status. That's what my racial group did when they/we used "God's will" to rationalize slavery, for example. It's like saying that poor people deserve to be poor.

Finally, my attention is drawn to the large-system level: organizations, institutions, systems of government, society at large, as I gear up to **deal with structural inequality & institutional racism.** I study how laws, regulations, policies, and practices perpetuate inequity and exclusion. I examine how culturally subordinated groups are impacted by the ways in which new technologies have reorganized the socio-economic system. The impact of this structural transformation is different depending on one's race, gender, and socio-economic status.

Subtler forms of discrimination have taken hold as various social forces (e.g. global economic interdependence, capital flight, the dominance of the information and service sectors) reinforce income inequality and wealth disparities. These patterns are deepening as new patterns of social-economic-political domination emerge*. Institutional racism is reproduced in new economic development, and every time that happens, the White-dominant cultural status quo gets even more entrenched.

As a leader, I can transform the basis of the system; for example, flattening unnecessary hierarchies in a managed way to foster equity and inclusion. I can lead and sponsor efforts to take down barriers to participation and performance that hinder the life chances of any culturally subordinated group members in my organization.

New law is needed at all levels for institutions to be more equitable and inclusive. New legislation and economic development need to reflect an equity-inclusion mindset

---

* Adapted from Zinn & Eitzen (2001).

or they will perpetuate structural inequality and institutional racism. How can I leverage my institutional roles in my various spheres of influence (e.g. work, church, children's school, civic organizations) to foster equity and inclusion?

The complexity of such large-system dynamics can feel overwhelming but I manage by changing only at the pace of insight; for example, by aligning my spending and giving practices with my values. I continue my learning journey at a pace with all sorts of social change aimed at educational, economic, and environmental justice. A daunting task, but partnering with both same- and different-race others to create more equitable social forms gives me strength and courage, especially in the face of resistance from those committed to preserving and expanding the status quo.

My learning and development is an incremental process of emerging awareness, skill-building, dealing with resistance, and occasional flashes of insight. I tolerate being consciously incompetent a lot of the time and appreciate those moments when I find myself competent around a skill that I've been practicing.

My relationships with other White People are getting stronger. We are more relational, less competitive, and less judgmental with each other. I'm more curious – asking questions, listening more – instead of feeling like I always need to know it all. If I'm a White Man, I'm more relational with other White Men for mutual support in the work that is uniquely ours. People of Color have been observing me during the Transition. They feel safer with me because they have seen me change how I connect with other White People. I'm being more honest, open, and accessible.

The winds of social change are blowing as I move toward the green section.

CHAPTER

seven

Equity & Inclusion (Green Section)

We have arrived at **Equity & Inclusion**, the green section on the Continuum. The relationship between People of Color and White People is structurally equitable in this domain, the race-color hierarchy undone, the categories themselves less meaningful.

We[*] see Equity & Inclusion social space as both reality and aspirational. We aspire to be equitable and inclusive as we work across the multiple social identity differences among us; at the same time, we usually find ourselves somewhere in the Transition. Still, over the years we have experienced many "green" moments among ourselves and in larger, mixed-race groups of colleagues. Synergy shimmers in such moments with a depth of mutuality that belies the racial divide.

Doing the work in the Transition has developed our[†] skills and made us more effective in our interactions across race difference. We hold ourselves as social equals: neither better-than nor less-than others, whatever our race-color might be. The "content of our character[‡]" has developed as well so that others are feeling the difference in us.

...WE DISCOVER PARTS OF OURSELVES AND ASPECTS OF OUR CULTURES OVER-SHADOWED BY DOMINANT GROUP/ SUBORDINATED GROUP SYSTEM DYNAMICS.

* The authors: Rick, Rianna, and Carol.

† From this point on, plural pronouns indicate both readers and authors, unless otherwise noted.

‡ From Dr. Martin Luther King, Jr.'s "I have a dream" speech on the National Mall, August 28, 1963.

When we encounter dominant/subordinated dynamics, we interrupt them. We create inclusive social spaces and ensure equitable access for everyone. We align our values-in-action (behavior) with our espoused values*.

We understand that everyone is both an individual and a member of a racial identity group; indeed, that everyone is a member of many social identity groups. We are all on multiple learning journeys out of dominant group and subordinated group statuses on other dimensions of diversity in addition to race-color. Our awareness of our respective multiple journeys establishes a nuanced social context as we enter the green section. Knowing that virtually everyone struggles with being one-down and less-than on some dimension of diversity gives us a fuller sense of our common humanity. We avoid competing for whose oppression is the worst, nor do we equate one system of oppression to another. We all strive to undo oppression where we find it while keeping our focus on undoing racism and racial inequality.

In addition, as *People of Color* in the green section, we strive to …

- claim space and experiment with moving into the center,
- explore the strength and beauty of our own cultures,
- stop assimilating to White culture,
- stop colluding in dominant group behavior toward other People of Color who are not members of our own race-color or ethnic identity group, and
- individualize White People in recognition of the work that some have done.

As *White People* in the green section, we strive to …

- share space, moving out of the center and making space,
- notice if we speak on behalf of one group of People of Color but not others,
- notice when we drop back into orange section behavior,
- own our culturally dominant group status and undo dominant behaviors

* Argyris, C. (1995).

- raise awareness among other White People of the implicit biases, stereotypes, and limits imposed by our socialization.

Besides mapping journeys at the individual and system levels, the Continuum maps the journey of the *intergroup relationship* between People of Color and White People. In the orange section, the relationship was injuriously fraught with tension, violence, and intense emotion; also, mutual dislike, disrespect, and distrust. In the Transition, the relationship improved incrementally as we worked on our respective learning journeys.

Once our journeys come together in the green section, **we discover parts of ourselves and aspects of our cultures that were overshadowed by dominant group/subordinated group system dynamics. This is true for everyone in the green section, irrespective of race-color difference.** We keep "doing the work" here, but now it is more about who we are and how we show up in social space, not merely what we do.

Entering the Green Section, from the Transition

As a Person of Color entering the green section, I am focused on developing a **self-defined racial-ethnic identity.** I need to have a robust sense of the value of my own humanity before I can safely join White People on a shared journey.

As a White Person, I am working on **listen**ing **without judgment.** Coming from genuine curiosity minimizes judgment and safeguards relationships. Others will only share the vulnerability of their journeys if they trust me, so non-judgmental listening is critical. This challenges me because White culture has set standards for what is right and true, so it is in the nature of Whiteness to always be an expert and authoritative on all things. Now I work at undoing my expectation that this is how the world is supposed to be so I can **consciously build relationships & community** with everyone. Experiencing different cultures broadens my horizons and enriches my life.

When Our Journeys Converge: Locations in the Green Section

Our first collaborative task is a cognitive one: to understand that **race is socially constructed.** It empowers us to know that 1) no arbitrary authority can force us to accept dominant-culture images, language, or narratives about race, race difference, or skin color, and 2) meanings are not set in stone. We have the power to deconstruct and reconstruct meanings as we see fit, via our social interactions and the outcomes of our collective learning. We make meaning *together*. This stance is what critical consciousness is all about. Paulo Friere called it liberatory practice*.

From our critical consciousness, we may decide that race itself is not a useful construct, or limit its use to specific contexts. The authors point to our own decision process about the identity designations used in this text to illustrate how this can work.

Identity Designations Used in this Text (from Chapter 2, pp. 24-25)

A racial identity designation for White People and geographic-ethnic designations (e.g. African American; American Indian; Iranian American, Latino/Latina) for People of Color are used here. Astute readers will pick up on the inconsistency so we want to be clear on the rationale for this usage….

- Although there is debate among People of Color about how to name themselves, a consensus has emerged in some communities to a) reject the race/skin color designations created by White People centuries ago and b) name themselves in terms of the geographic and ethnic origins of their people.

- Whiteness is the binding force among persons from many geographic/ethnic origins in the world. It is the phenomenon encountered by non-White persons across the US, whether they were born here or immigrated. Since White People socially constructed "Whiteness" for ourselves to begin with, we are lying in a bed of our own device and dealing with it, right here and now.

---

* Freire, P. (1968).

We effectively brought critical consciousness to the race construct and liberated our collective consciousness in this decision process.

Equity and inclusion is created in all our spheres of influence as we adopt the attitudes and practice the skills in the green section, and as a result, civil society at-large aligns incrementally with the greenspace vision. My competency is crucial in this process so I commit to continued learning and ongoing self-development, moving in stages from unconscious incompetence to unconscious competence*.

A Step Learning & Competency Development Model

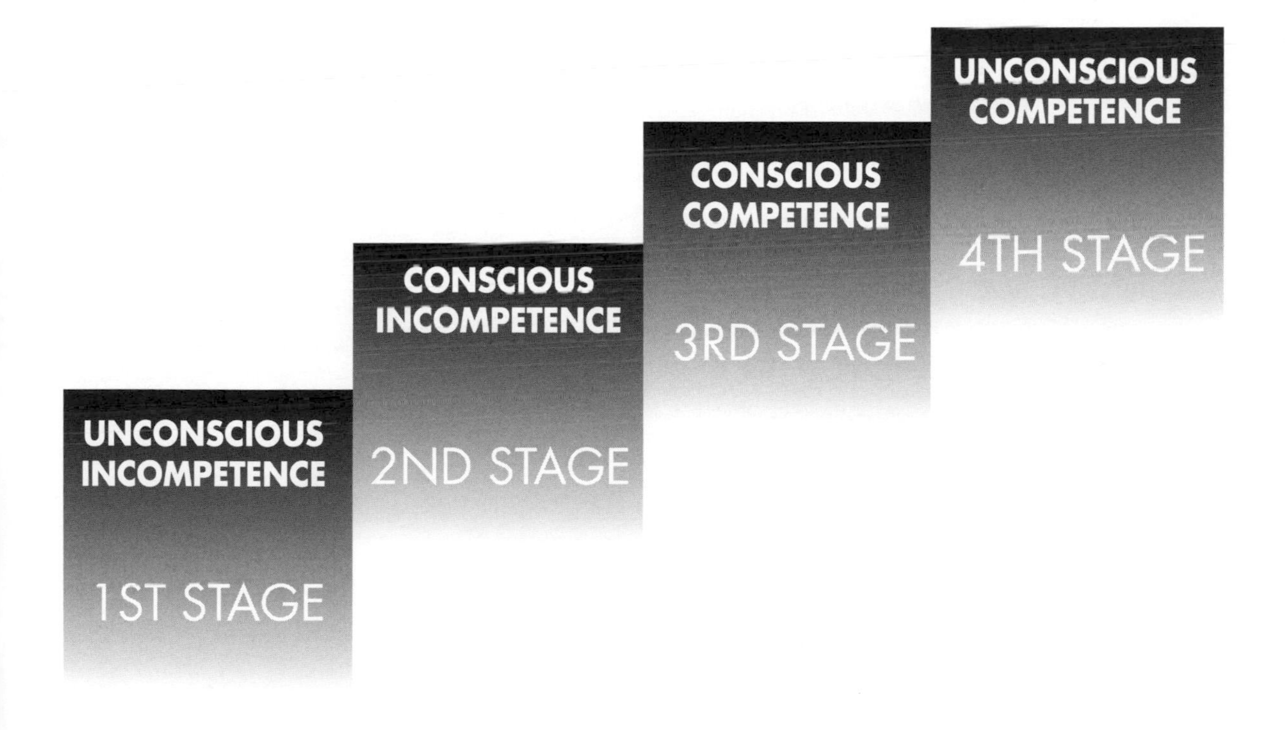

* Based on a model created by Noel Burch at Wilson Learning in the mid-1970s. Note that the First Stage correlates roughly to the orange section on the Continuum; the Second Stage to the late orange/early blue; the Third Stage to the early blue through late blue; and the Fourth Stage to the green section.

1st Stage: Unconscious Incompetence. *I don't know what I don't know.*	The race problem is a sad, regrettable part of history but it's behind us now. • I treat everyone the same; I don't even see race or color. • I avoid others who are a different race. We should keep to our own. • Racism has not affected me personally. I wish people would get over it, stop looking back. • All anyone needs to succeed is to pull themselves up by their boot straps. • I don't understand why she won't be my friend, just because I'm White and she's Penobscot. We're all the same under the skin!
2nd Stage: Conscious Incompetence. *Uh-oh … now I know what I don't know!*	Something happens to make me aware of how much I don't know. • I'm a PoC*, shocked to find a racial slur spray-painted on my locker, or to find out that everyone else in my cohort has been promoted and is paid more than I am; frightened to find a noose hanging on my car in the parking lot after work; sickened when the n-word is scrawled on the wall in the hallway as I leave the orchestra pit. • I'm a WP, hurt when a PoC colleague confronts me about "forgetting" to acknowledge his contribution to a project which he attributes to my racism, or stunned when a PoC woman colleague points out how WW always expect to be kept comfortable or refuses my friendship because I'm so unconscious of my Whiteness.
3rd Stage: Conscious Competence. *I know what I know but I need to pay attention constantly!*	I understand more now and have some skills. I pay attention to what I'm doing and to my impact. I am wary and afraid of making a mistake. • In unfamiliar social contexts, even if I think I know the "right" way to behave, I own my awkwardness, confusion, or fear but do not lead from them. • I stay open to learning and keep taking risks and practicing. • I ask for feedback from both same- and different-race others, especially around my blind spots.
4th Stage: Unconscious Competence. *It's second nature for me now.*	My sense of myself has transformed. I often do the right thing without having to think about it. I feel more confident around different-race others. • I engage productively in conflict with different-race others and facilitate others in conflict across race difference; I can handle guilt, shame, anger, and fear; I self-disclose appropriately to build relationship. • Others lean on me for support on their learning journeys. • I lead social change/social justice initiatives in my spheres of influence. • I set expectations for behavior change toward equity & inclusion and hold others accountable with 360 feedback processes. I support their development with coaching and affinity groups.

We are still doing the work but are also **being the work** in the green section: being the change we want to see in the world†. It's about the quality of our being in our daily

* PoC = People or Person of Color; WP = White People or Person; WW = White Woman.

† "Be the change you want to see in the world" is a paraphrase of a longer quote from Gandhi.

walk, whatever institutional roles we hold. Use of Self is a critical dimension of the change agent's repertoire because who we are and how we show up in social space determines how capable we are of influence of change. Am I integrated and congruent, or am I conflicted, disorganized, and disconnected from my authentic self?

Philosophers since ancient times, therapists and psychoanalysts since Freud, and sociologists since George Herbert Mead have explored the concept of self. I am both changer and changed as I use my self to influence the world while the world influences and shapes me. All subsequent locations in the green section should be viewed through a Use-of-Self lens.

"Self" is ...

- a compelling sense of our unique existence or personal identity
- an inner agent or force that controls and directs fear and other emotions
- the inner witness to events
- a synthesis of an organized whole having a continuity of life experience over time; or personality*
- a mix of character attributes, needs and motives, intentions, styles, habits, and defenses†
- It develops as we interact with others in relationship throughout the lifespan‡.

When we are at odds with each other because our needs or perspectives are different, we don't pretend that everything is fine. We stay with the tension and proactively ***use* conflict to develop skills & build relationship.** We track the origins of conflict and leverage the self-awareness and interpersonal skills we've built to engage in dialogue. *People of Color* no longer excuse *White People* by projecting benevolent intent. We hold them accountable for their impact and give them feedback; likewise, *White People* give honest performance feedback to *People of Color* or feedback on their impact in social space.

---

* Reber, 1985, pp. 675-676.

† Seashore, Shawver, Thompson, & Mattare (2004), p. 44.

‡ Jordan, J.V., Walker, M., & Hartling, L.M. (2004).

Use of Self – Capabilities and Qualities for Creating Equity & Inclusion

- a *capacity* for showing up and being fully present in social space, irrespective of comfort level
- an *awareness* of my projections and stereotypes about different-race others and the ability to manage myself around them
- a *commitment* to healing from the earlier parts of our journeys and transforming how we relate to each other as we collaborate across race difference
- *knowing* what my triggers are and how to manage myself around them
- the *ability* to ride the emotional energy wave of someone else's impact from something I've said or done without feeling guilty or defensive, even when I'm full of emotion from being confronted about my impact on the other person
- *clarity* about how to facilitate change at all levels of system. I have the agency needed to carry out courses of action, and I trust my ability to influence without controlling
- the *ability* to apply what I have learned about emotional and social intelligences in my work and personal life

It may feel awkward but we trust each other to hang in and work it through. We own our experience, including the impact we are sitting with in response to what others have said or done. We own our projections and emotions to avoid labels and judgments. We listen respectfully. We use the Continuum to examine our behavior and motivations. If we find ourselves back at an earlier location on the Continuum, we share what we have unearthed and trust the other person to hold our vulnerability. Each time we do this, more trust is built and another chunk of racial inequality undone.

In our organizations and teams, we **attend to both content & process.** The *content* task is *what* we are doing. The *process* concerns *how* we go about the content task. Dominant group/subordinated group system dynamics are latent in every social context, whether it is a mixed-race group or not, so a work group's process is always affected by them. If process is ignored, effectiveness and productivity suffer.

Often unconscious of how we act around others, we can be flustered at times by the impact of our speech or other behavior. In green social space, we understand that impact matters hugely. Feedback helps us calibrate between our behavior and impact.

We **seek & appreciate diverse perspectives** in our teams and community groups because we understand that it serves the common good to do so. Productivity increases when diversity is present, *if* it is optimized by ensuring that all voices are heard and various

Could Feedback Help? Real-Life Mini-Cases to Illustrate Inequitable/Oppressive Racial Dynamics

- A Person of Color contributes an idea but is ignored or interrupted by a White Person. Later, a White Person presents the idea and receives recognition.
- Most of the air time is taken up by the White People in the room.
- Some People of Color are criticized for not making eye contact or for not being assertive, outspoken, loud, or self-aggrandizing enough … while others are criticized for being too loud, expansive, self-aggrandizing, etc.
- People of Color are asked to represent and speak for their group or community*.
- A Person of Color and a White Person collaborate on a project. When the White Person makes the presentation, only her name is on the slides.
- White members regularly confuse the names of the Women of Color on the team, laughing each time it happens. The confusion is never resolved.
- The word "black" is used to signify negativity or evil.
- Frustrated with an African American tech's performance, a White supervisor says "If you don't get up to speed on this, I'll have to crack the whip"†

* At the same time, People of Color need to be acknowledged and supported when they want to speak on behalf of their identity group or community. They just need to say that's what they are doing.

† "Crack the whip" means to behave in a domineering way toward subordinates; to demand obedience, hard work, or efficiency from others in a harsh manner. The term carries racially incendiary connotations because the plantation overseer "cracked" a bull whip to terrorize field laborers and keep them in line.

inputs considered in the development of solutions. I make my best contribution when my own **support systems & networks reflect diversity.** Persons who used to be absent from my networks and support systems are present now, bringing energy and excitement into my work and life.

As diversity increases in our organizations and communities, it is normal to feel uncomfortable at times. Our worldviews are challenged. Things are less predictable but we are okay with it because we know that **discomfort & ambiguity are the norm.**

As we move among different race-color groups, we tolerate discomfort brought by a wider range of emotions, from fascination to affection and attraction to confusion, uncertainty, and fear. We dig for the origin of our anxiety to understand and take better care of ourselves without pushing it out onto others. If we tire from being pushed about our impact, we take a timeout to reflect and renew. When we feel like walking away, we stay put longer to find out what happens and see what can be learned.

Sometimes it's not easy being "green" for any of us, whatever our race-color. *For me as a White person*, it's often about feeling how not in control I am. It takes energy to lean into uncertainty and ambiguity, and it's especially difficult if I have not ventured outside U.S. White-dominant culture much. It's hard to not be paralyzed. Understanding how White culture is different from other cultures helps a lot. I want to develop at least a degree of biculturalism so I can function better in People of Color cultures, whether in the US or abroad.

Many of People of Color cultures are more group- and community-oriented, less organized around individual striving than I'm used to, so it's a stretch but if I stay with it, I find that I'm enjoying myself. Likewise, when I allow things to emerge organically, I discover that there are other ways of dealing with life than what I've been used to. I realize that I've got some skills when I notice myself actively participating in other cultures without causing disruption. That feels good.

I find People of Color who are centered in their own reality and beyond the need to punish White People, so they are willing to be open and honest with me. I also find other White People who are working at getting it, even though we may not be doing it at the pace that People of Color might wish for.

For me as a Person of Color, the engine driving the discomfort is different from what goes on for White People. It's not about fear. What it is about is my realization that *all* of us are working on these skills in the green section, so none of us is exactly comfortable. We are all somewhat uncomfortable *and* we share a commitment to the values and principles of this space. We are all seeing each other and working together at all levels of system. When we are working together, I can hold you (White Person) as an individual member of the White group, and I can hold us in the context of the whole system of which we are members. The fact that we are uncomfortable doesn't mean that good work isn't going on. In fact, some degree of discomfort probably means the opposite, that good work *is* going on.

Ambiguity is normal for everyone. Multiple viable realities exist in the midst of great complexity, so there are a lot of moving parts. My ability to tolerate ambiguity develops as I engage across race difference. Speaking my ambivalence out loud is an effective Use of Self because it facilitates insight for me and offers access to others.

I've been practicing and am now **willing to give & receive feedback across race difference.** I don't allow ambiguity or uncertainty to stop me. Most of us are not comfortable with or skilled at feedback to begin with, so we tend to avoid it, and race difference exacerbates discomfort. I practice giving feedback without judgment. I also ask for feedback and expand my capacity for receiving it. It's the best tool available to me for understanding my impact.

Historically, People of Color have not given feedback to White People because it is too risky, but *as a Person of Color* in the green section, I need to manage my anxiety and other emotions when asked to give feedback to a White Person. I also need to take the risk of asking a White Person for feedback so I can listen, learn, and develop.

As a White Person, I am leery of *giving* People of Color feedback because I'm afraid of doing something wrong. I'm anxious about *asking* for feedback from a Person of Color but 1) I need to hear it for my own development, and 2) they need to hear White People say that they are valued for who they are, what they bring, and what their insights and observations are, so I push through my resistance and ask.

As I move deeper into the green section, I am constantly scanning myself in social space **(scan self-in-system)**: How do I feel; what am I thinking; do I know anyone here? What does my racial identity mean in this context? More **aware of context** now, I track which social identity groups are present and whether any "onlies" are present. Am I an only? How does an only affect group dynamics? Are the onlies present members of a culturally dominant group or a culturally subordinated group?

I track purpose, agenda, roles, and what has been left undone. I'm aware of the energy in the room and tracking who is doing most of the talking or controlling the meeting. I track dynamics across race difference happening at both interpersonal and intergroup levels. I notice if historical patterns of racial dynamics seem to be playing out and

Real-Life Examples of Intragroup Dynamics

- White-collar Anglo-Saxon White Men control the agenda, compete with each other, take up all the air time and make comments about the clothing and appearance of the blue-collar ethnic White Women present, who sit silently throughout.
- Self-identified Spanish Americans talk about not letting their children date "Mexicans" from south of the border. They do not seek input from the Mexican Americans on the team, who are silent.
- Persons of African descent from Jamaica and the Azores ignore the African Americans present but ridicule their speech, making jokes about "Ebonics, mon!"

how sub-groups of People of Color and White People are interacting. The Use-of-Self skill involved here is to notice without judgment or interpretation. I'm observing and collecting data about the system from the system itself. The data will be useful if I decide to intervene.

Soon I find myself being called to **step into leadership to undo racism.** My interpersonal effectiveness and ability to facilitate conflict and dialogue across race difference has been noticed by others in my workplace, school, community, or place of worship. They feel safe talking about race in my presence. Leadership is a matter of the influence I have, irrespective of my title or formal role. I have influence when I notice and name racist speech or behavior. I track and name less-than messages about any race-color group, including my own.

As a White Person in a room where only White People are present, I influence when I intervene, sometimes with only a quiet observation or question. *As a Person of Color,* I pay attention so I do not unconsciously internalize less-than messages.

Stepping into Leadership

- A White supervisor wants coaching on how to give developmental feedback to a Person of Color.
- An African American supervisor is anxious about demoting a White employee and wants help thinking and feeling it through, and for making a plan for the meeting with the employee.
- An Asian American executive is aware that no Latino/Latina or African American has ever been promoted into a senior management position in her division. She wonders if she herself may be reinforcing barriers to entry, however unintentionally, and wants to explore this possibility.
- People of Color in the congregation have been avoiding the White pastor. He asks for help in understanding what the issues with him or his leadership might be.
- The pastors of all the churches in my city are collaborating to foster ecumenicism and community. They are a mixed-race group and need some process consultation as they try to work equitably but are hampered by hierarchical impulses. They ask me to facilitate the needful conversations.

People of Color and White People alike are responsible for tracking and naming dysfunctional patterns in micro-moments like these. If I hold a formal leadership role, I am concerned about these patterns being so embedded in the organization's culture that they damage morale, increase undesirable attrition, bring negative attention to the organization, and contribute to a drop-off in productivity. It is incumbent on me to be tracking, naming, and dealing with racism and structural inequality.

All the locations on the green loop are aspects of effective leadership and Use of Self toward creating equity and inclusion. I step into leadership when I practice these behaviors. If I have not yet practiced them, trying to step into leadership at this point will lack substance and integrity. Others will not have faith in my ability to lead social change because they have not already witnessed me stepping into leadership and using my self effectively. If this is the case (feedback can tell me if it is), I need to reboot. I find another journeyer to coach and mentor me.

The final location on the green spiral is **Facilitative Presence.** Presence is an energetic phenomenon, its quality measured by what it evokes in others. What do I want my presence to evoke? I look to the teachers, mentors, and role models who have supported my journey so far. What has their presence evoked in me? How has it facilitated my learning, risk-taking, personal growth and professional development, and leadership? Mastery is a given. I appreciate the integral and congruent nature of their competence: their knowledge base, skills, and Use of Self[*].

The other critical factor is *psychological and emotional safety.* I have felt safe enough in their presence to work at my learning and growing edges where I am least competent and feel most psychologically-emotionally vulnerable, the moments in which danger signals are flashing in my psyche. The presence of my teachers and mentors has facilitated my ability to hold myself at those edges; to stay present and learn despite discomfort and anxiety in those intense moments.

---

* Moore, R., & Huntley, R. (2011).

Two key qualities of their presence foster safety. One is that *they don't judge* me. They accept me where I am. They've worked along the rough edges of fear, anger, judgment, and projection in their own psyches, so they know what it takes to hold oneself on those edges to optimize for learning and development. This leads to the second element, which is that they have become *role models* because of the work they've done. I watch what they do, I listen, I ask about their practice – why they made this choice in that situation and not a different one. What were they thinking; how were they feeling in that moment? How do they deal with intense emotion and defensiveness? And so on.

So: I want others to feel safe enough with me to learn and do their work. I want them to take courage from my presence. I want to *be*, and *be seen as*, values-oriented, personally integrated, and competent. I want my presence to support others being where they are at the same time as they see me standing in a place that is different from theirs and modeling a different way of being.

I also want my presence to facilitate a shift in the whole system. I walk in the energy of the system *but differentiate myself from it.* As my presence facilitates others and their work, the social spaces I show up in become more equitable and inclusive. Equity enhances the sense of belonging for others and fosters trust. It doesn't mean that we agree. Rather, equity and inclusion help make it safer for us to differentiate ourselves and deal productively with differences and conflict.

Developing a facilitative presence also requires me to tune into what is *evoked in me* when I share social space with other persons whose race-and-color is different from my own. The latent gifts of my humanity begin to develop when others' diversities show up in my world to evoke them. When I see with my heart and open to something beyond the self, my facilitative presence is enhanced.

CHAPTER

eight

Conclusion

We come back to Use of Self to conclude our discussion of the Continuum. It is no accident that Use of Self comes early in the green section as well as here, at the end of the journey. In the end, the journey is about learning, dialoguing across race difference, and influencing change at all levels of system, through our Use of Self.

Families, friendships, primary relationships; the workplace, a place of worship, a school, neighborhood, civic organizations, or government entities: all are sites in which we can use ourselves to create equity and practice inclusion. Yes, we learn some basic skills, but then like jazz artists we improvise as we go because there is no race work playbook, script, or recipe. The effectiveness of our activism – how skillful we are at leading and influencing social change for the highest good of all concerned – depends on us: who we are, what skills we bring to the table, and how we use our selves.

THE RACE PROBLEM IS COMPLEX BUT WE ARE CALLED TO DO THE WORK, REGARDLESS; TO BE THE CHANGE, REGARDLESS.

The self is developed through social interaction, so being face-to-face at some point is necessary for learning beyond the cognitive level. Experiential learning laboratories* provide a safe container for deepening self-knowledge, interacting across race difference, and increasing awareness of the impact of one's behavior. If things don't go the way we had intended, hoped, or expected, we don't give up. We keep on keeping on, embracing "failure" as a powerful vehicle for learning, becoming more self-aware, and enhancing our skills. As Winston Churchill once said, we need to go from "failure to failure with enthusiasm".

We need to be aware of our fears and triggers, and manage ourselves around them so they do not paralyze us or lead us to act out in ways that harm us or others. We need to know our values, character, personality, motivations, learning styles, knowledge bases, skillsets, and the impact of family of origin on our development. How was race talked about in the house? How were emotions dealt with?

It is the journey of a lifetime to know the self, but deepening our self-knowledge by listening to feedback, learning how to work with system energy†, and continuing to do our inner work enhances the quality of our facilitative presence and our leadership. More and more, we embody the change we wish to see in the world.

Walking the Talk

The parallel positioning of our journeys as People of Color and White People portrays our interrelatedness and encourages intergroup dialogue. We need to talk, engage constructively, and move from vision to action. We dialogue to bridge our differences, ease the tensions between us, and advance mutual understanding in interpersonal and group encounters.

We (the authors) see ourselves in dialogue with you, going forward. We have made the first dialogic move by offering this book and the Continuum, and you have

---

* NTL Institute for Applied Behavioral Science (www.ntl.org) offers research-based social justice-oriented experiential learning programs, coaching, and consultation.

† Moore, R., & Huntley, R. (2011).

responded by reading and engaging with it. Thank you for coming with us all this way.

Skills for Dialogue

Creating a satisfying and mutually respectful dialogue across race difference asks us to …

- remember that both interpersonal and intergroup levels are always present in the same moment
- use "I" language and avoid "you" statements
- share experience instead of opinions and judgments
- track emotions and self-manage around them to be appropriate for the context
- seek first to understand, check out assumptions, and practice empathy
- sustain a conversation thread by listening to and building on others' contributions, responding to others' questions, using air time wisely
- pay attention to the impact of our behavior, assume the benevolence of others' intentions, and continue engaging when the impact of our actions is different from what we had intended.

Doing the Work and Being the Change

When you are whitewater rafting, you can take your boat right up to a monster wave rushing over a massive boulder jutting out from the middle of the river. If all the rafters paddle hard enough in coordinated fashion, the boat can be held right up against the wave so everyone feels the rush. The subconscious takes in innumerable clues about what's happening all around while the prow of the raft pushes into the face of tons of surging hydropower. Focus and skill keep the boat upright and catastrophe at bay. Amid the roar, ordinary reality is transcended. You are exultant.

Doing race work at our learning and growing edges can sometimes feel like that. Authentic dialogue and engagement across race-color difference can feel like that. We are pushing into the face of a powerful cultural status quo that has existed for nearly four hundred years. We are working to ride and redirect that flow, to avoid being swamped or overturned, and any work we do at any level of system in any of our spheres of influence is going to impact the whole of it.

The race problem is complex but we are called to do the work, regardless; to be the change, regardless. Denial, avoidance, and minimization perpetuate the status quo, but authentic dialogue across race difference without judgment, blame, or shame helps undo racism and moves us toward actualizing the vision of Equity & Inclusion.

We can do this.

REFERENCES

Argyris, C. (1995). *Organizational learning II: Theory, method, and practice.* Upper Saddle River, NJ: FT Press.

Banaji, M.R., & Greenwald, A.G. (2013): Blindspot: Hidden biases of good people. New York, NY: Random House.

Bonilla-Silva, E. (2001). *White supremacy and racism in the post-Civil Rights era.* Boulder, CO: Lynne Reiner Publishers.

Buchanan, N.T. (2005). "The nexus of race and gender domination: The racialized sexual harassment of African American women". In Morgan, P., & Gruber, J. (Eds.). In the company of men: *Re-discovering the links between sexual harassment and male domination (pp. 294-320).* Boston, MA: Northeastern University Press.

Frankenberg, R. (1993). *The social construction of whiteness: White women, race matters.* Minneapolis, MN: University of Minnesota.

Gergen, K. (1994). *Realities and relationships: Soundings in social construction.* Cambridge, MA: Harvard University.

Goleman, D. (1995). *Emotional intelligence.* New York: Bantam.

Gould, S.J. (1984/1996). *The mismeasure of man.* New York, NY: W.W. Norton.

Habermas, J. (2001). *On the pragmatics of social interaction: Preliminary studies in the theory of communicative action* (B. Fuller, Trans.). Cambridge, MA: MIT Press.

Hardiman, R. (1982). "White identity development: A process oriented model for describing the racial consciousness of White Americans." Doctoral dissertation. Scholarworks @UMass Amherst.

Helms, J. (1995). "An update of Helms's White and People of Color racial identity models". In Ponterotto, J.G., Casas, J.M., Suzuki, C.A., & Alexander, C.M. (Eds.). *Handbook of multi-cultural counseling* (pp. 181-198). Thousand Oaks, CA: Sage.

Holvino, E. (2006). "Tired of choosing": Working with the simultaneity of race, gender, and class in organizations. *CGO Insights, 24.*

Jordan, J.V., Walker, M., & Hartling, L.M. (2004). *The complexity of connection: Writings from the Stone Center's Jean Baker Miller Training Institute.* New York, NY: The Guilford Press.

McIntosh, P. (1988). White privilege and male privilege: A personal account of coming to see correspondence through work in women's studies. In Anderson, M.L., & Collins, P.H. (Eds.). *Race, class, and gender: An anthology* (pp. 95-105). Belmont, MA: Wadsworth-Thomson Learning.

Miller, J.B. (1976). *Toward a new psychology of women.* Boston: Beacon.

Moore, R., & Huntley, R. (2011). Understanding and using system energy. *Practising Social Change, 4.*

Pierce, C., Wagner, D., & Page, W. (1986/2004). *A male/female continuum.* Laconia, NH: New Dynamics Publications.

Reber, (1985). *The Penguin dictionary of psychology.* New York: Penguin.

Rosenblum & Travis (2012). *The meaning of difference: American constructions of race, sex and gender, social class, sexual orientation, and disability.* Columbus, OH: McGraw-Hill.

Thomas, L., & Pierce, C. (1988). *A black/white continuum in white culture: Paths to valuing diversity.* (Graphic.) Laconia, NH: New Dynamics Publications.

Thomas, L., & Pierce, C., with Huntley, R., Washington, S.B., Wagner, D., & Joseph, L. (1999). *Journeys of race & culture: Paths to valuing diversity.* (Graphic.) Laconia, NH: New Dynamics Publications.

Van Dijk, T. (1987). *Communicating racism: Ethnic prejudice in thought and talk.* Newbury Park, CA: Sage.

Wishik, H., & Pierce, C. (1995). *Sexual orientation & identity: Heterosexual, Lesbian, Gay, & Bisexual journeys.* (Graphic.) Laconia, NH: newdynamics Publications.

Zinn, H. (1980/1999). *A people's history of the United States, 1492-present.* New York, NY: HarperCollins.

Zinn, M.B., & Eitzen, S.D.(2000). In conflict and order: Understanding society. Boston, MA: Allyn & Bacon.

Zuberi & Bonilla-Silva. (2008). *White logic, white methods: Racism and methodology.* Lanham, MD: Rowman & Littlefield.

SUGGESTED READING

This list is not meant to be exhaustive but as a place to begin.

Orange Section: Cultural Dominance & Subordination/Racial Inequality

Personal Narratives and Fictions

Many of these narratives document the experience of living in culturally subordinated group status as Person(s) of Color. A few are written by White People coming to critical consciousness about Whiteness and their own White identity.

Alexie, S. *Any of his novels. Sherman Alexie is Spokane-Coeur D'Alene indigenous American.*

Asian Women United. (Eds.). (1989). Making waves: *An anthology of writings by and about Asian American women.* Boston: Beacon.

Baldwin, J. (1955). *Notes of a native son. Boston: Beacon. James Baldwin (1924-1987) was an American novelist, essayist, playwright, poet, and social critic. All his novels are recommended.*

Bataille, G.M. (1989). *American Indian women telling their lives.* Lincoln, NE: University of Nebraska Press.

Berlin, I., Favreau, M., & Miller, S.F. Miller (Eds.). (1998). Remembering slavery. New York, NY: The New Press.

Berry, W. (1989/2010). *The hidden wound.* New York, NY: North Point Press. *A powerful essay about racism and the damage it has done to the author himself as an individual White Man as well as to the country as a whole.*

Brown, D. (1973). *Bury my heart at wounded knee: An Indian history of the American west.* New York, NY: Bantam Books. *A classic.*

Coates, T. (2016). *Between the world and me.* New York, NY: Spiegel & Grau. *A contemporary African American man's letter to his son – an examination of the hazards and hopes of Black male life in America.*

Deloria, V., Jr. (1969). *Custer died for your sins: An Indian manifesto.* New York, NY: Avon Books. *A classic.*

Dyson, M.E. (2017). *Tears we cannot stop: A sermon to White America.* New York, NY: St. Martin's Press.

Ellison, R. (1962). *Invisible man.* New York, NY: Random House.

Fong-Torres, B. (1994). *The rice room: Growing up Chinese-American: From number two son to rock & roll.* New York, NY: Hyperion.

Gomez, A., Moraga, C., & Romo-Carmona, M. (1983). *Cuento: Stories by Latinas.* New York, NY: Kitchen Table – Women of Color Press.

Green, R., & Porter, F.W. Porter (Eds.) (1992). *Women in American Indian society: Indians of North America.* New York, NY: Chelsea House Publisher.

Hughes, L. (1934/1962). *The ways of white folks.* New York, NY: Random House.

Irving, D. (2016). *Waking up white and finding myself in the story of race.* Chicago, IL: Elephant Room Press.

Jacobs, H. (1859/1973). *Incidents in the life of a slave girl* (first published under the pseudonym Linda Brent). San Diego, CA: Harcourt Brace.

Lorde, A. (1994/2007). *Sister outsider.* Berkeley, CA: Crossing Press. *See essay titled "The Master's Tools Will Never Dismantle the Master's House".*

Manlapaz, E.Z. (Ed.). (1994). *Songs of ourselves.* Santa Monica, CA: Philippine American Literary House.

Mihesuah, D. (1996). *American Indians: stereotypes & realities*. Atlanta, GA: Clarity Press.

Mirandi, A., & Enriquez, E. (1979). *La Chicana: The Mexican-American woman.* Chicago, IL: University of Chicago Press.

Momaday, N.S. (1968). *House made of dawn.* New York, NY: Harper.

Moraga, C., & Anzaldua, G. (Eds.) (1983). *This bridge called my back: Writings by radical women of color.* New York, NY: Kitchen Table: Women of Color Press.

Northup, S. (1853). *Twelve years a slave.* Mineola, NY: Dover Publications.

Okubo, K. (2013). *Japanese mother.* Collins Publishing. Available on Amazon.

Steiner, S. (1968). *The new Indian.* New York, NY: Harper & Row. *A classic.*

Styron, W. (1967). *The confessions of Nat Turner.* New York, NY: Random House.

Walker, A. (1982). *The color purple.* New York, NY: Rodopi Press.

Walker, R. (2001). *Black, white, and Jewish: Autobiography of a shifting self.* New York, NY: Penguin.

Wright, R. (1940). *Native Son.* New York, NY: Perennial (HarperCollins).

Yan, Y. (2006). *White like me: New Americans, new promise: A guide to the refugee journey in America.* Saint Paul, MN: Fieldstone Alliance Publishers.

Critical Theory, Analysis, & History

Anderson, C. (2016). *White rage: The unspoken truth of our racial divide.* New York, NY: Bloomsburg. *Redirects some of the White peoccupation with Black rage.*

Christian, C.M., & Bennett, S. (1995/1999) *Black saga: The African American experience (a chronology).* New York, NY: Basic Books.

De Gruy, J. (2005). *Post traumatic slave syndrome.* Portland, OR: Uptown Press.

Gould, S.J. (1984/1996). *The mismeasure of man.* New York, NY: W.W. Norton.

Hacker, A. (1992). *Two nations: Black and white, separate, hostile, and unequal.* New York, NY: Macmillan.

Isenberg, N. (2006). *White trash: The 400-year untold history of class in America.* New York, NY: Viking.

Kovel, J. (1971). *White racism: A psychohistory.* New York NY: Vintage. *A classic.*

Kumar, D. (2012). *Islamophobia and the politics of empire.* Chicago: Haymarket Books.

Miller, J.B. (1976/1987). *Toward a new psychology of women.* Boston, MA: Beacon. *A modern classic – the theoretical foundation for cultural dominance/subordinated group & system dynamics.*

Mills, C.W. (1997). *The racial contract.* Ithaca, NY: Cornel University Press.

Morrison, T. (Ed.) (1992). *Race-ing justice, en-gender-ing power: Essays on Anita Hill, Clarence Thomas, and the construction of social reality.* New York, NY: Pantheon Books.

Painter, N. (2010). *The history of white people.* New York, NY: W.W. Norton.

Said, E. (1979). *Orientalism.* New York, NY: Vintage. *A classic.*

Walker, A. (1982). *The color purple.* San Diego, CA: Harcourt.

Wilkerson, I. (2010). *The warmth of other suns: 1915-1970.* New York, NY: Random House. *About African Americans' Great Migration, from the South to the North.*

Blue Section: Transition

Personal Narratives and Fictions

These narratives and fictions reflect what it feels like to step forward into the Transition as a time of learning and social change for individuals leaving culturally dominant status or culturally subordinated status behind.

Ali, A.H. (2010). *Nomad: From Islam to America – A Personal Journey Through the Clash of Civilizations.* Houston, TX: Free Press.

Anzaldua, G. (Ed.). (1990). *Making face, making soul: Creative and critical perspectives by women of color.* San Francisco: CA: an aunt lute foundation book.

McIntosh, P. (1989). "White privilege and male privilege: A personal account of coming to see correspondences through work in Women's Studies". Downloadable pdf available @ www.nationalseedproject.org.

Morgan, S.L., & De Wolfe, T.N. (2012). *Gather at the table: The healing journey of a daughter of slavery and a son of the slave trade.* Boston: Beacon.

Weincek, H. (1999). *The Hairstons: An American family in black and white*. New York, NY: St. Martin's Press.

Wise, T. (2011). *White like me: Reflections on race from a privileged son.* Berkeley, CA: Soft Skull Press.

Zia, H. (2000). *Asian American dreams: The emergence of an American people.* New York, NY: Macmillan.

Critical Theory, Analysis, & History

Albrecht, L., & Brewer, R.M. (Eds.). (1990). *Bridges of power: Women's multicultural alliances.* Philadelphia, PA: New Society Publishers. Published in cooperation with the National Women's Studies Association.

Alexander, M. (2012). *The new Jim Crow: Mass incarceration in the age of colorblindness.* New York, NY: The New Press.

Asian Women United of California, Ed. (1989). *Making waves: An anthology of writings by and about Asian American women.* Boston: Beacon Press.

Frankenburg, R. (1993). *The social construction of whiteness: White women, race matters*. Minneapolis, MN: University of Minnesota.

Goleman, D. (1997). *Emotional Intelligence: Why it can matter more than IQ.* New York, NY: Bantam Books.

hooks, b. (2013). *Writing beyond race: Living theory and practice.* New York, NY: Routledge

Katz, J.H. (2003). (25th Anniv. Ed.) *White Awareness: A handbook for anti-racism training.* Troy, NY: KJCG.

Kochman, T. (1981). *Black and white styles in conflict.* Chicago: University of Chicago.

Kumar, D. (2012). *Islamophobia and the politics of empire.* Chicago: Haymarket Books.

Schaefer, C., Amundsen, K., & Tarcher, J. (1993). *Creating communication anywhere: Support and connection in a fragmented world.* Los Angeles, CA: Perigee Books.

West, C. (1993). *Race matters.* Boston: Beacon Press.

Zinn, H. (1980/1999). *A People's History of the United States, 1492–Present.* New York, NY: HarperCollins.

Green Section: Equity & Inclusion

These works theorize about more equitable less hierarchical social structures, offering suggestions on how to be more interpersonally effective and productive in such structures.

Block, P. (2008). *Community: The structure of belonging.* San Francisco, CA: Berrett-Koehler.

Bolen, J.S. (1999). *The millionth circle: How to change ourselves and the world.* Boston, MA: Conari Press.

Diamond, L. (2001). *The peace book: 108 ways to create a more peaceful world.* Berkeley, CA: Conari Press.

Helgeson, S. (1995). *The web of inclusion: Building an organization for everyone.* New York, NY: Doubleday.

Howard, D. (2006). *Repairing the quilt of humanity.* Silver Spring, MD: Beckham Publications Group.

Katzenbach, J.R., & Smith, D.K. (1992). *The wisdom of teams: Creating the high-performance organization.* Cambridge, MA: Harvard Business School Press.

Litwin, A. (2014). *New rules for women: Revolutionizing the way women work together.* Annapolis, MD: Third Bridge Press.

Moore, R., & Huntley, R. (2016). Designing a better box for Gallese, Italy: Diversity-inclusion and social power in a global context. *OD Practitioner*, October 2106.

Moore, R. & Huntley, R. (2011). Understanding and using system energy. *OD Practitioner, 4,* pp. 4-10.

Olson, E.H., & Eoyang, G.H. (2001). *Facilitating organizational change: Lessons from complexity science.* Hoboken, NJ: Wiley.

Owen, H. (2008). *Open space technology: A user's guide.* Potomac, MD: Abbott.

Owen, H. (1997). *Expanding our now: The story of open-space technology.* San Francisco, CA: Berrett-Koehler.

Pierce, C. (1988/2011). *The power equity group: A guide for understanding equity and acknowledging diversity.* Laconia, NH: New Dynamics Publications.

Pierce, C. (2002). *"Power equity group theory: A new frame of reference for OD". OD Practitioner, 34,* 3, p. 27.

Pierce, C., & Moore, R. (2008). Power equity group theory: A review for practitioners. *OD Practitioner, 40,* 3, p. 31.

Pipher, M. (2003). *The middle of everywhere: Helping refugees enter the American community.* New York, NY: Harcourt Books.

Putnam, R.D., & Feldstein, L.M. (2003). *Better together: Restoring the American community.* New York, NY: Simon & Schuster.

Surowiecki, J. (2004). *The wisdom of crowds.* New York, NY: Doubleday.

Watkins, J.M. & Mohr, B.J. (2001). *Appreciative inquiry: Change at the speed of imagination.* San Francisco, CA: Jossey-Bass/Pfeiffer.

Wheatley, M.J. & Kellman-Rogers, M. (1996). *A simpler way.* San Francisco, CA: Berrett-Koehler.

Wheatley, M.J. (1992). *Leadership and the new science: Learning about organizations from an orderly universe.* San Francisco, CA: Berrett-Koehler.

Yousafzae, M., with Lamb, C. (2015). *I am Malala.* New York, NY: Back Bay Books/ Little Brown.

ABOUT US

The authors ...

Rick Huntley is a highly skilled leadership and change consultant, coach, and teacher with demonstrated ability to facilitate learning and skill development using group development theory and experiential learning to develop the client's core skills for leading across race, gender, and other dimensions of difference. Rick consults to labor, healthcare, medical research, and in the government sector.

A member of NTL Institute for Applied Behavioral Science since 2003, Rick was for many years on the faculty of two of the organization's signature programs designed to develop practitioner skills for facilitating interpersonal and group-level learning and development in NTL's Human Interaction Labs. He was a managing faculty member for NTL's Diversity Leadership Certificate Program and served as Chair of NTL's Board of Directors from 2012 through 2014.

A few of Rick's recent publications include "Designing a Better Box for Gallese, Italy: Diversity/Inclusion and Social Power in a Global Context" *(OD Practitioner;* October 2016), and "Understanding and Using System Energy" (*Practicing Social Change;* November 2011), both with Rianna Moore.

As a member of the faculty for the American University Masters of Organization Development Program (Washington, DC), Rick taught Group Theory and Change Facilitation, and currently co-facilitates Learning Community Time in that program. He also taught in the Executive Certificate in Strategic Diversity and Inclusion Management at Georgetown University's Continuing and Professional Education Program.

Rick completed graduate study at Howard University in Washington, DC; did his undergraduate study at Morgan State University's School of Social Work in Baltimore City; and earned a post-graduate certificate in Organization and Systems Development from the Gestalt OSD Center in Cleveland. He is an award-winning speaker with Toastmasters International.

Rianna Moore, PhD, is a veteran OD practitioner, author, and diversity-inclusion specialist. A member of NTL Institute since 1998, Dr. Moore leads NTL's Publishing Hub and contributes to the Core Labs and Research & Writing Hubs. Dr. Moore is faculty for NTL's signature Human Interaction (H.I.) Lab as well as for the program that qualifies other members to staff the H.I. and other Core Labs. In addition, she consults on customized solutions for NTL's client systems.

Dr. Moore staffs the *Power Equity Group in Theory & Practice* lab for New Dynamics and other diversity/inclusion learning laboratories focused on power and privilege on various dimensions of diversity, including race and gender. She is involved in several research and writing projects that reflect on various aspects of practice. Recent publications include "Designing a Better Box for Gallese, Italy: Diversity-Inclusion and Social Power in a Global Context" (*OD Practitioner;* October 2016), "Understanding and Using System Energy" (*Practising Social Change;* November 2011), both with Rick Huntley; also, "Power Equity Group Theory: A Review for Practitioners". *OD Practitioner, 40,* 3, p. 31, with Carol Pierce.

Dr. Moore has worked with client systems in the corporate, government, and higher education sectors. Her corporate career included a tour as the Director of OD & Diversity for Global Manufacturing & Engineering and management development specialist for a Fortune 50 high-tech firm. She has conducted consulting projects and professional development programs in Italy, Russia, Germany, Scotland, Canada, Nationalist China, and throughout the US. Dr. Moore taught at several universities in the northeastern US prior to her OD consulting career, including Norwich University (VT) and the State University of New York (SUNY Fredonia). She holds a Masters in OD and the PhD in Human & Organization Systems from the Fielding Graduate University; also a Masters in English from SUNY Fredonia.

Dr. Moore is a member of the American Association of University Women, the League of Women Voters, the NAACP, and the Southern Poverty Law Center.

Carol Pierce founded new*dynamics*, an organization development firm, in 1972. She created new*dynamics* Publications in 1986. Her specialties are diversity consulting and training, process consultation, and strategic planning in flatter, less hierarchical structure. She has worked with a variety of client systems in business, industry, human service, health, education, and religious institutions for over 40 years.

Ms. Pierce is an innovator in the field of diversity education, when there were few professional diversity training programs and little published material for corporate consulting. Along with diverse colleagues, she is a designer of programs and writer in the areas of gender, race and culture, and sexual orientation, as well as the use of egalitarian structure where power equity, partnership, and creativity are important. She is the innovator of Power Equity Group (PEG) theory, a major contribution to the field of Applied Behavioral Science. It validates and facilitates the understanding of egalitarian structure. In a PEG, naturally appearing experiential energy is acknowledged when diversity and its impact on groups is recognized and understood.

Ms. Pierce provides leadership and support to change processes resulting from the influx of refugees in her community and across the United States. In 2000, along with the Police Chief, she created a Mayor's committee dedicated to valuing cultural diversity in Laconia (NH) and cultivating a community-wide climate that does not tolerate prejudice or discrimination of any kind. She has facilitated the resettlement of refugees and welcoming of immigrants for 16 years. She brings together immigrants, professional staff from local human service and educational organizations, and the police to support resettlement.

She is a member of the NTL Institute for Applied Behavioral Science. She serves on community boards and/or committees: Genesis Behavioral Health in central New Hampshire, the New Hampshire Endowment for Health, and the New Hampshire Women's Foundation. She is a graduate of the University of Wisconsin School of Music and the Organization & Systems Development program at the Gestalt OSD Center in Cleveland.

New Dynamics....

New Dynamics *helps organizations recognize and ameliorate the effects of implicit/unconscious biases about other people based on race, color, sex/gender, class, ethnic origins, religion, sexual orientation, and other social differences. We developed the widely recognized "journey" Continuum models that guide individuals from behaviors that perpetuate systems of oppression to new ways of relating that make each person powerful and whole. Our Continuum models have become the backbone for the work of other practitioners. Our approach is largely experiential and based on the understanding that lasting change addresses issues at the individual, group, and whole system levels.*

We offer laboratory education programs based on our journey models in partnership with NTL Institute for Applied Behavioral Science (www.ntl.org).

New Dynamics Publications....

New Dynamics Publications newdynamic@aol.com *is a voice for persons of diverse genders, races, colors, cultures, and callings who experience life as a creative journey. In partnership with NTL Institute for Applied Behavioral Science, we publish expressions of the search for meaning and knowledge creation, including social science research.*